Photographing California

Dennis Ariza

Copyright © 2022 Dennis Ariza

All rights reserved. This publication, or any part thereof, may not be reproduced in any form, or by any means, including electronic, photographic, or mechanical, or by any sound recording system, or by any device for storage and retrieval of information, without the written permission of the copyright owner.

Dedication

I dedicate this book to Annelle, the love of my life.

Contents

1. Mono Lake 1
2. Lundy Canyon 4
3. Chemung Goldmine 5
4. Bodie State Park 7
5. Death Valley 14
6. Alabama Hills 16
7. Yosemite National Park 19
8. Sacramento Valley National Wildlife Refudge 22
9. Colusa Wildlife Refudge 25
10. Lassen National Park 26
11. Hat Creek Area 28
12. Pit River Area 31
13. Mccloud River 33
14. Dunsmuir Area 35
15. Point Reyes National Seashore 39
16. Muir Woods National Monument 45
17. Santa Cruz Area 47
18. Elkhorn Slough 49
19. Hallberg Butterfly Garden 53

20 Ironstone Winery 55

21. Uvas Canyon Regional Park 59

22. Carson Pass Area 62

About the Author 67

About the Book 68

1. Mono Lake

The Eastern Sierra has a variety of locations to photograph. These locations do require an overnight stay. I make my home base in the town of Lee Vining, California, near Mono Lake, where I am centrally located amid Yosemite, Death Valley, the Chemung Gold Mine, and Bodie State Park. I normally stay three or four nights.

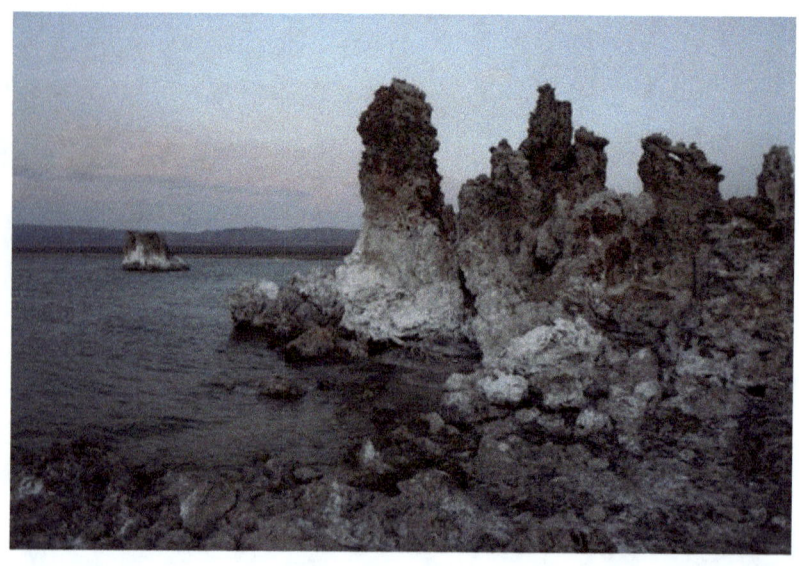

The South Tufa on Mono Lake offers a beautiful place to photograph in the early morning for a lovely sunrise shot and late afternoon for a beautiful sunset shot. In the late spring/early summer, shots of the tufa with the snow-covered mountains in the background can be absolutely amazing. East of the South Tufa is Navy Beach, a location where the federal government and the navy conducted weapons experiments and tested propellers for their fleet. The facility was operational from 1950 until it was closed in 1962. It is also the location of the Sand Tufa. The sand tufa was created when water is heated by magma and rises to the surface depositing fine sand particles.

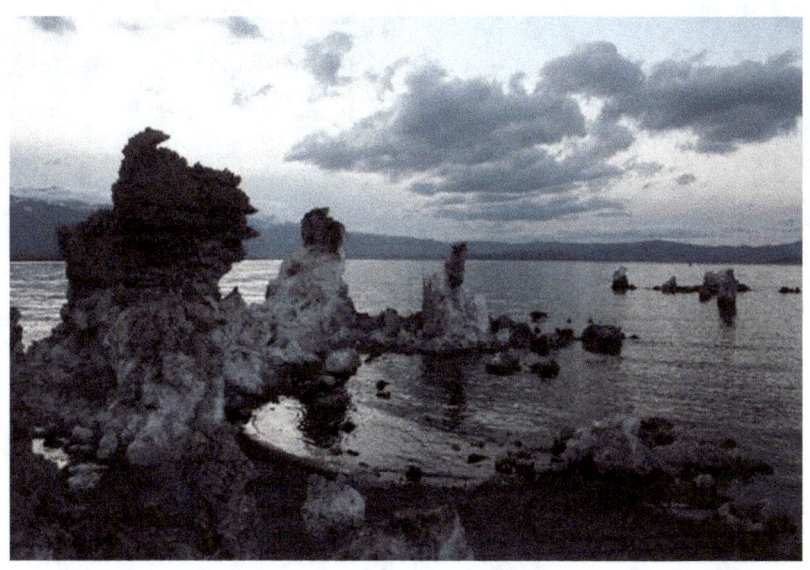

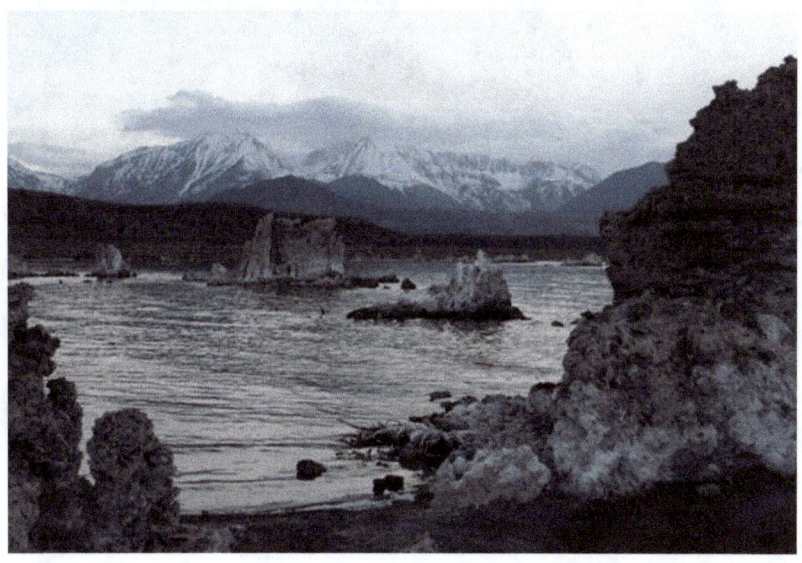

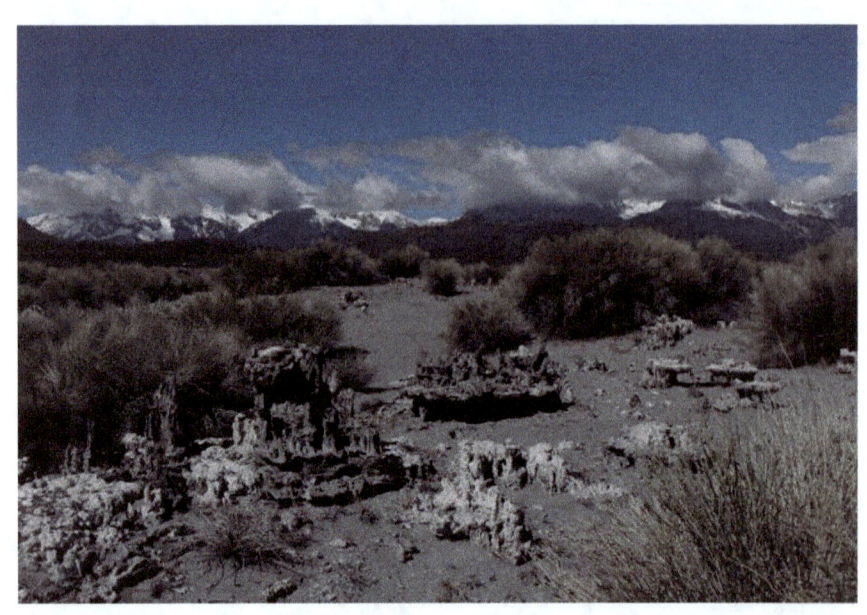

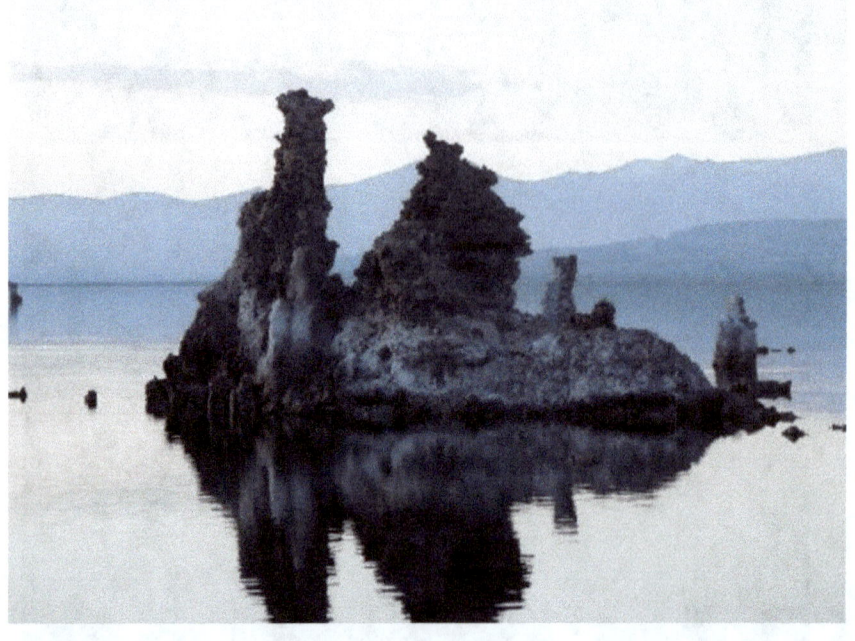

2. Lundy Canyon

Lundy Canyon is a small fishing resort just northwest of Mono Lake and Highway 395. Lundy Lake is a small man-made lake that is a popular trout fishing area. Lundy Canyon is west of the lake and is famous for wildflowers and wildlife photography. The Lundy Creek is home to many beaver, hawks, deer, and golden eagles. At the west end of the canyon, there is a large waterfall that feeds the largest of the beaver ponds on the creek. I never realized how large the dam was until I was standing at its base. The top of the dam was over my head. If that dam had broken, I could have been washed away. In the late spring early summer after the snow melts, it is also a great location for wildflowers.

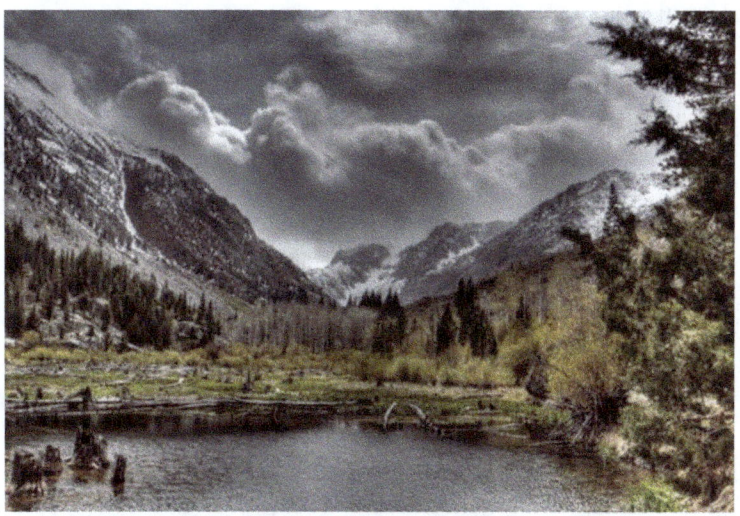

3. Chemung Goldmine

The Chemung Gold Mine located in Mono County, California, operated from 1909 to 1938. It closed when the cost of hauling the gold to Bodie became too much for the little mine. During its run, it processed over a million dollars' worth of gold. During the 1920s, the mine produced low- and high-quality ore. The mine did not close because of the lack of gold, but because of poor management. During its time of operation, management built three different mills and tore them down. The mine was reopened in the late 1950s to the mid-1960s by a loan prospector, "Heinie" Heinmeyer. Today some of the gold processing equipment still stands, but a large amount of the equipment has been removed. The mine was located near the town of Masonic.

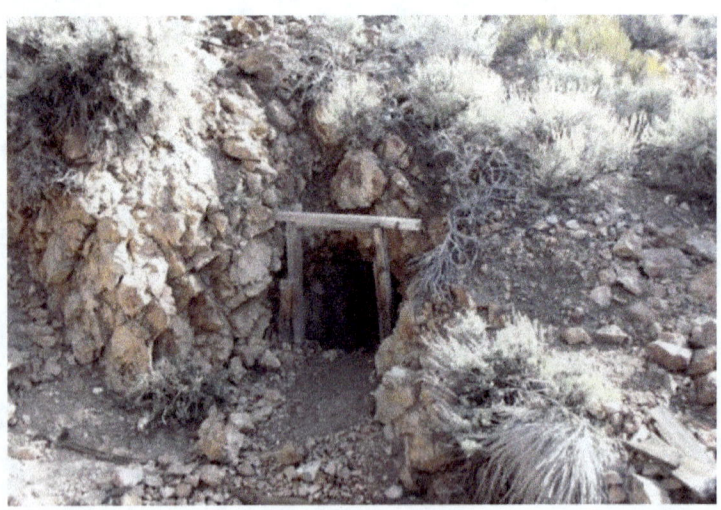

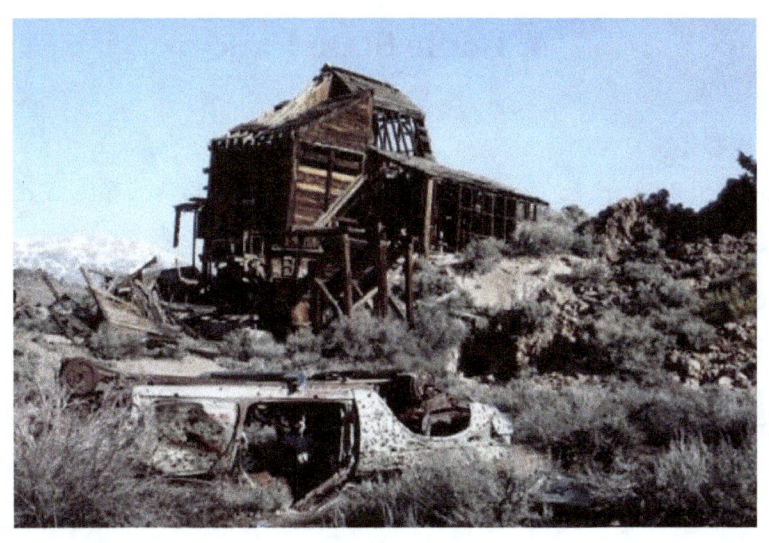

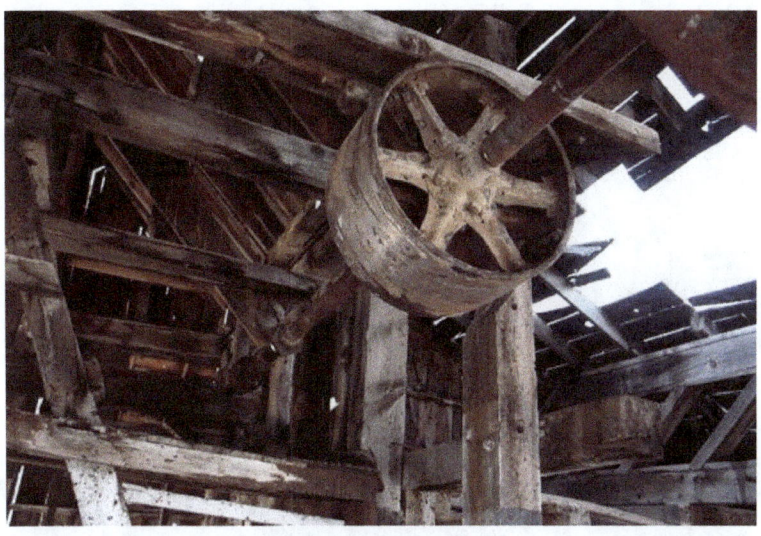

4. Bodie State Park

Bodie State Park is located in the Eastern Sierras, seventeen miles east of Highway 395 and south of Bridgeport, California. In 1859, Samuel (A.K.A. Waterman) S. Bodey discovered gold in what is now known as the Bodie Bluffs. In 1861, a mill was built, and the town began to grow. The town began with a group of twenty miners and by 1880 had grown to over 10,300 people. The town was known to consist of over sixty-five bars at its peak and have its own red-light district several blocks long.

In 1962, the state of California designated Bodie as a state park. The buildings were not restored and are preserved in the condition they were found "Arrested Decay."

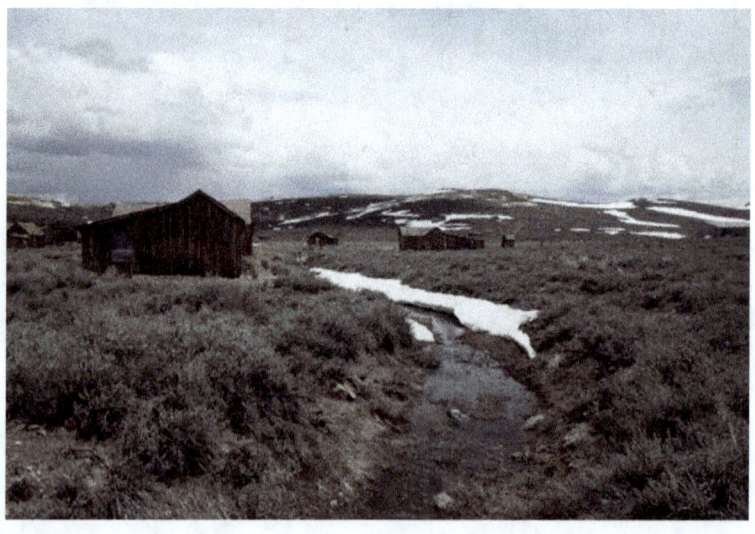

Above are some of items for sale on the shelves at the General Store including Hills Brothers Coffee. The General Store offered a complete line of mining equipment, guns, pots, pans, food, and clothing.

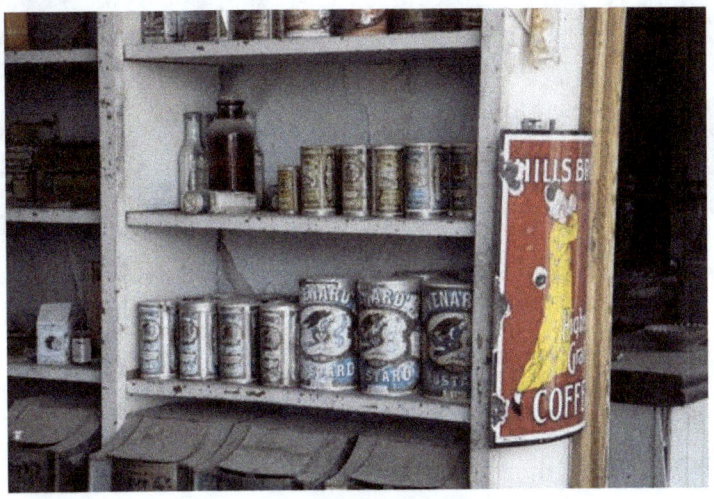

General Store

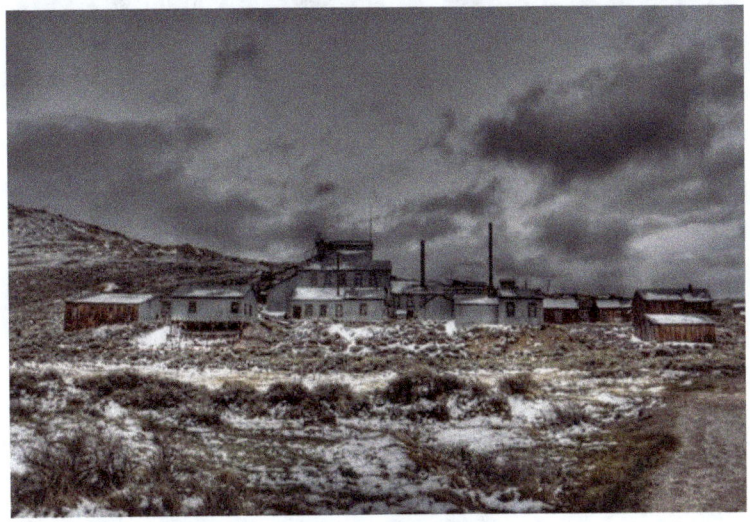

Bodie Gold Mine

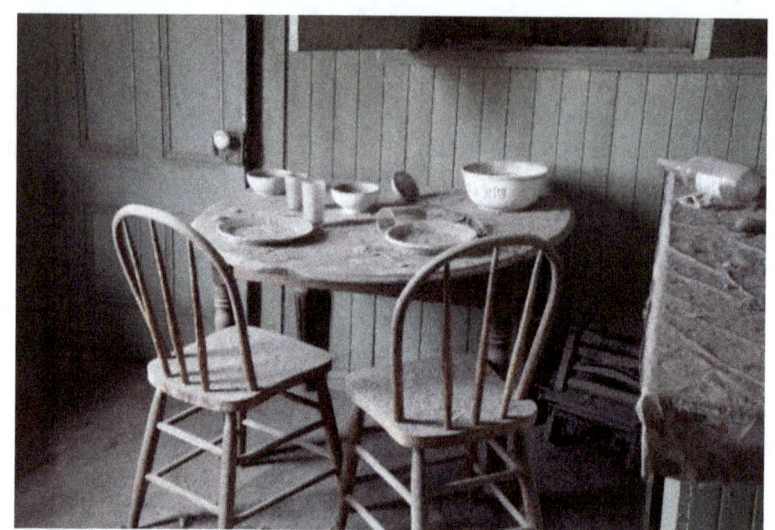

It is said that a group wanted a sign to welcome people to "Bodey," but they hired someone from out of the area to create the sign. When the sign arrived, he had spelled the name "Bodie," and the name has stuck ever since.

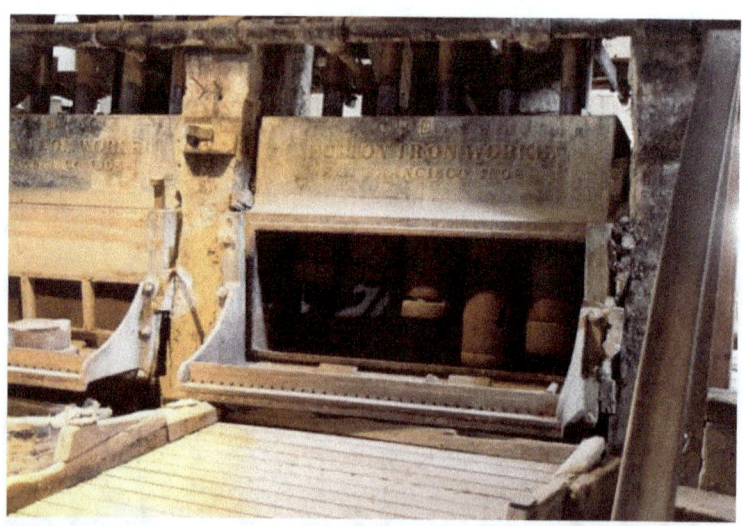

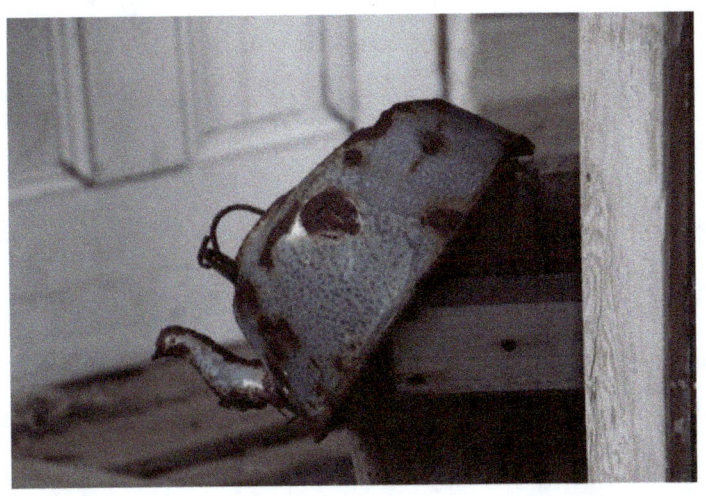

When the mill opened in 1861, it consisted of twenty gold stamps. The stamps would move up and down and crush the ore with each stroke. It was said that the crushing sound of the stamps would shake the entire town at night.

To maintain the gold stamp and all the mills equipment, a machine shop was needed to cast and repair replacement parts.

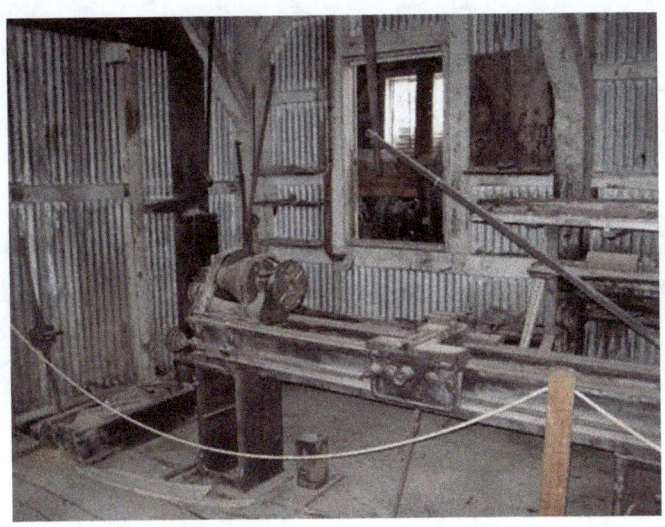

Visiting Bodie

Bodie is normally snowed in with up to fifteen feet of snow each winter. Park rangers park their vehicles just off Highway 395 and use snow cats to travel in and out of the park for supplies. The road into Bodie opens in late April or early May.

Members of the Bodie Foundation along with the State Park Services celebrate Bodie Days the first weekend of August. The Park Service opens most of the buildings. There is a parade, art show, BBQ, and music. The surviving residents return and are dressed along with Park Rangers as they were in the era when the gold mine closed in 1954. This is the Bodie Foundations largest fundraiser. For additional information about "Bodie," please purchase my book, "Bodie, A Ghost Town."

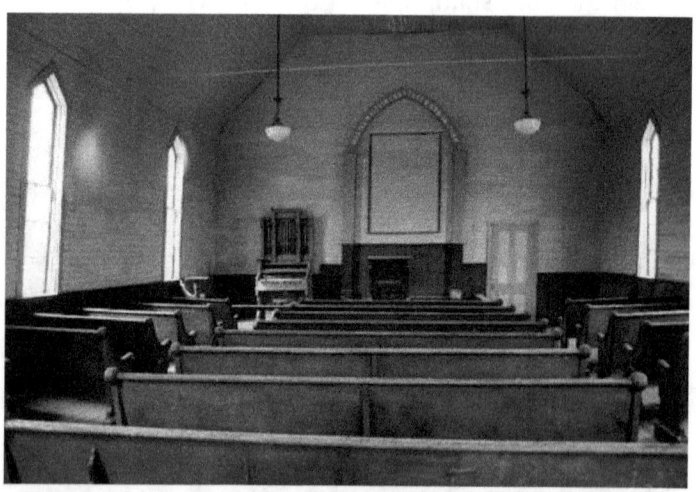

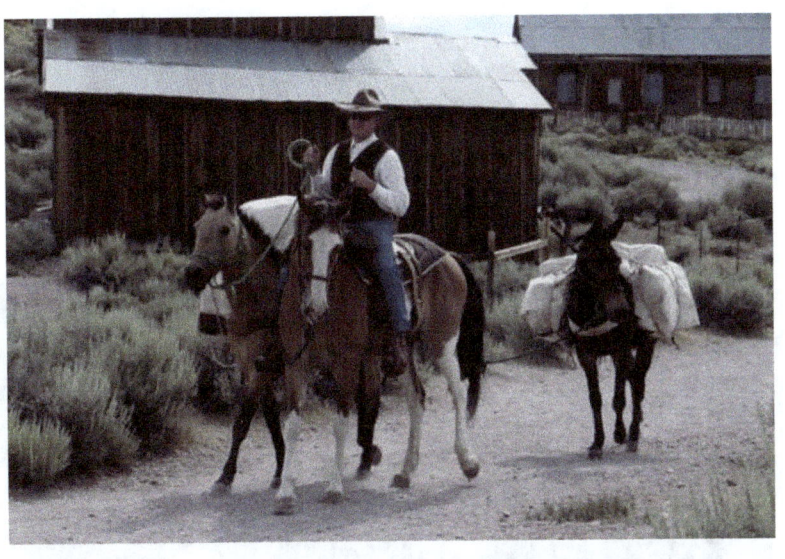

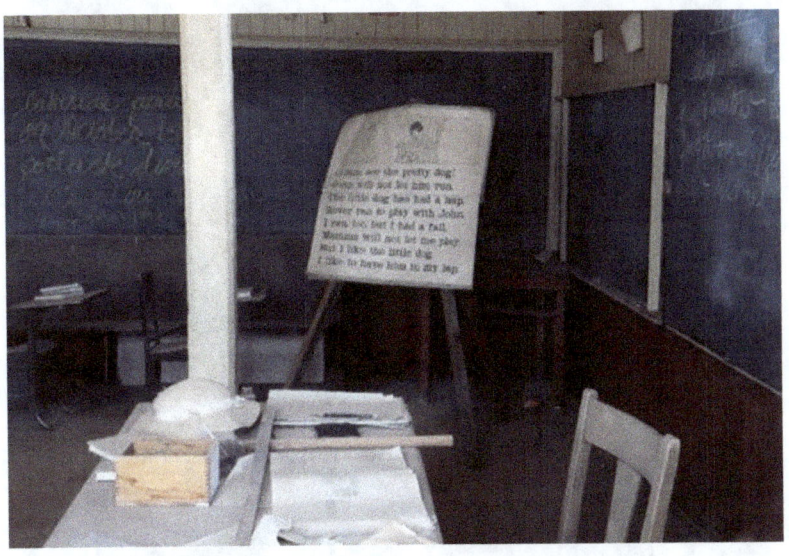

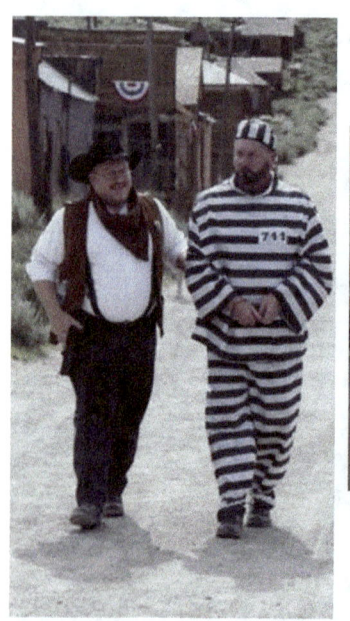
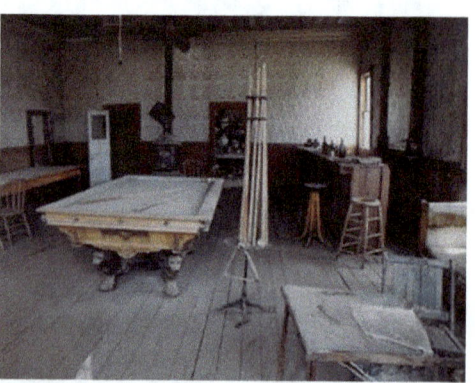
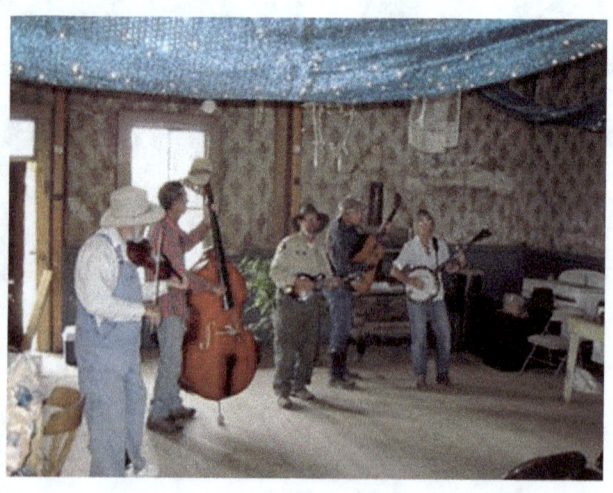

5. Death Valley

One of the few places to stay in Death Valley is Stovepipe Wells. I have been staying there since my second trip to Death Valley and used it as my base camp. It was much cheaper and gave me more time to explore the area. Staying outside the park can add over an hour of travel each way to the park.

Mesquite Dunes

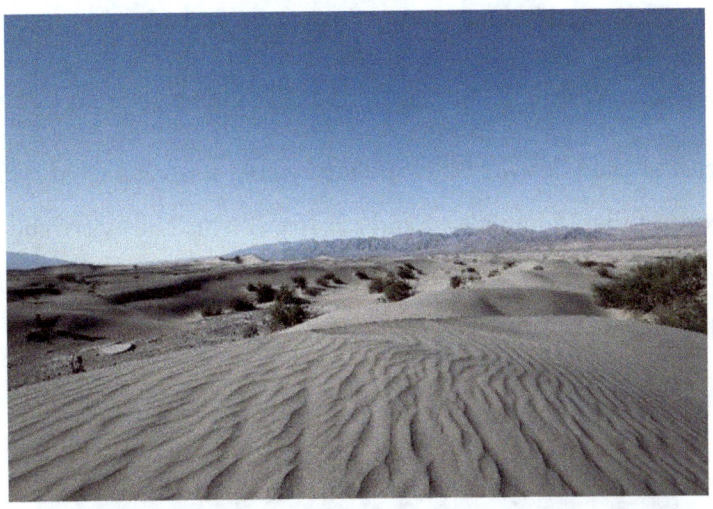

Across from the hotel are the Mesquite Dunes that stretch for miles. In the early morning hours, it was a great location for animal tracks before the breeze came up and destroyed them.

Racetrack

Racetrack is known for its rocks that magically move across the playa. For thousands of years these rocks have been moving slowly across the playa leaving a trail in the mud. The road on the way there is a deep cut washboard one lane narrow gravel road. On the way there on the gravel road, I noticed something running ahead of me.

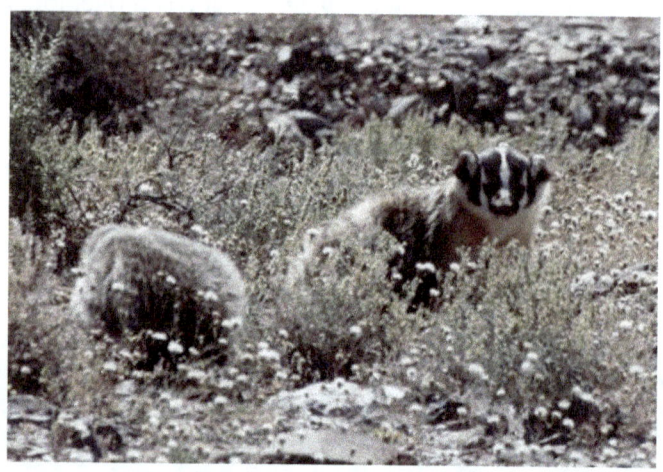

When I slowed down and let the dust settle, I saw a pair of badgers in front of me. I jumped out and ran after them. They were ahead of me and ran very fast. At one point, they stopped to see if I was still behind them and that was when I took the shot on the left.

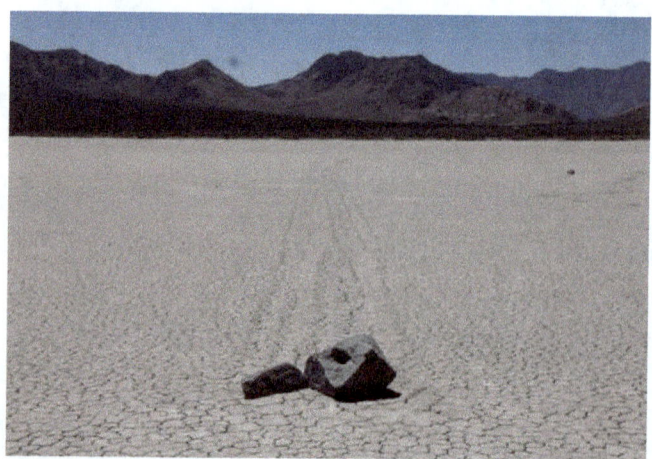

6. Alabama Hills

Located off the Mount Whitney Portal Road, north of Lone Pine, California. They are famous for their beauty and for all the movies and televisions shows that have been filmed there. Actors and actresses like John Wayne, Spencer Tracey, Steve McQueen, Elizabeth Montgomery, George Kennedy, and Maureen O'Hara have made hundreds of movies there, not to mention television shows like the Lone Ranger, Have Gun will Travel and episodes of Bonanza.

The welcome rock at the entrance to the Alabama Hills.

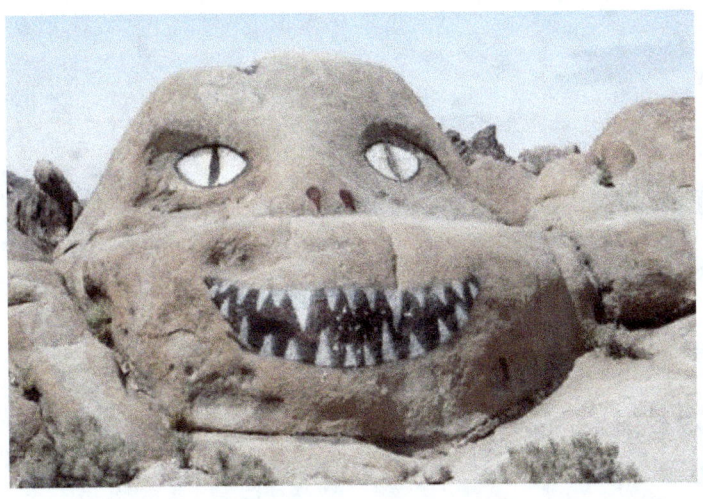

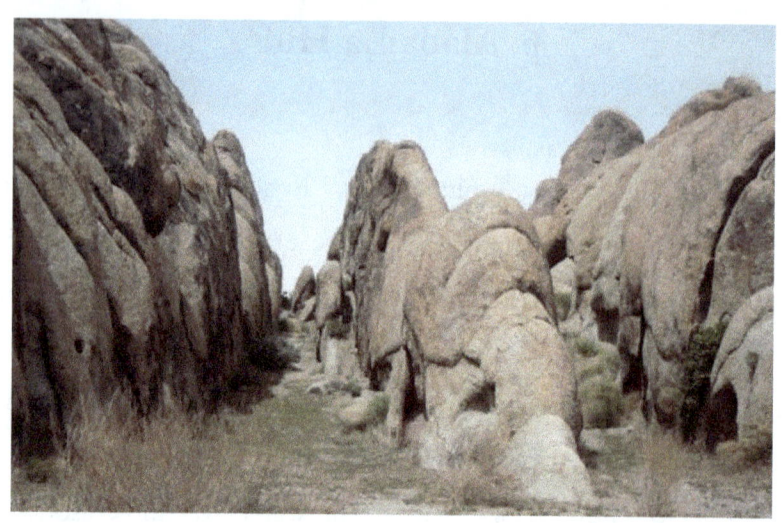

Canyon used by the Hole in the Wall Gang in "Butch Cassidy & the Sundance Kid." One of the most recent popular movies filmed in the Alabama Hills was "Iron Man" starring Robert Downey, Jr.

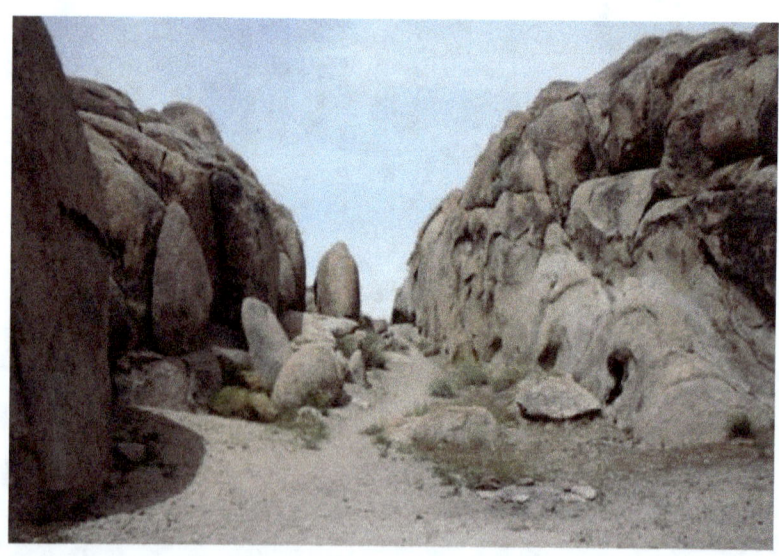

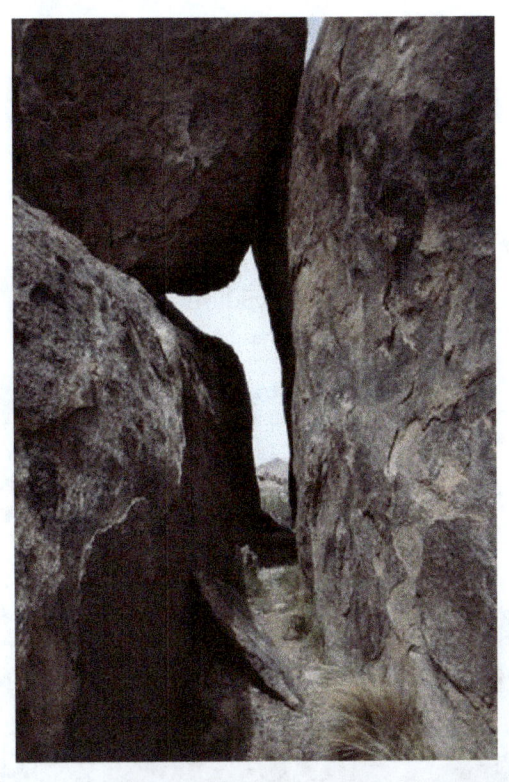

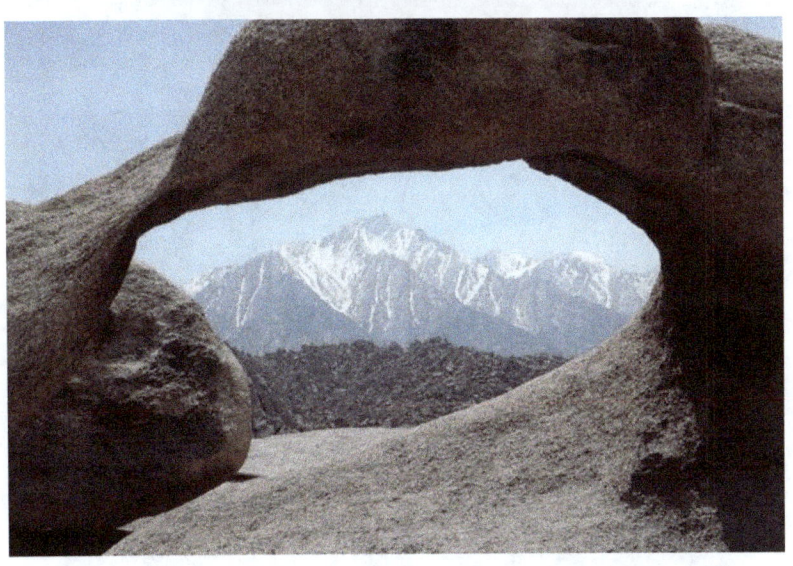

7. Yosemite National Park

Yosemite National Park established in 1864 contains deep valleys, grand meadows, granite formations, vast wilderness, lakes, streams, waterfalls, and an abundance of wildlife.

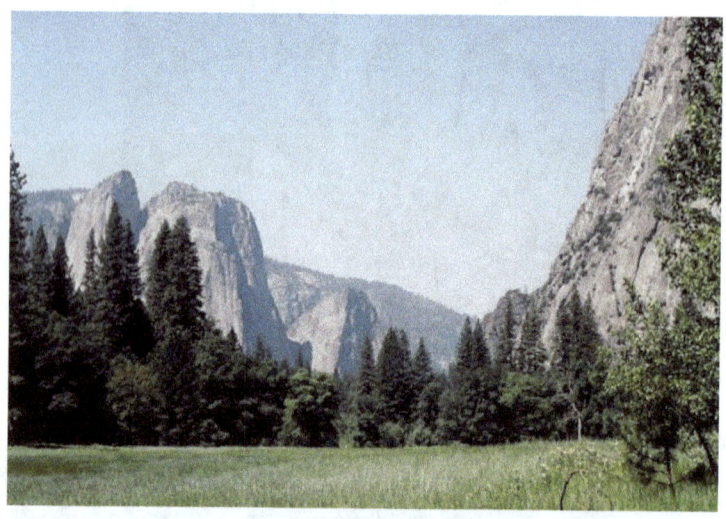

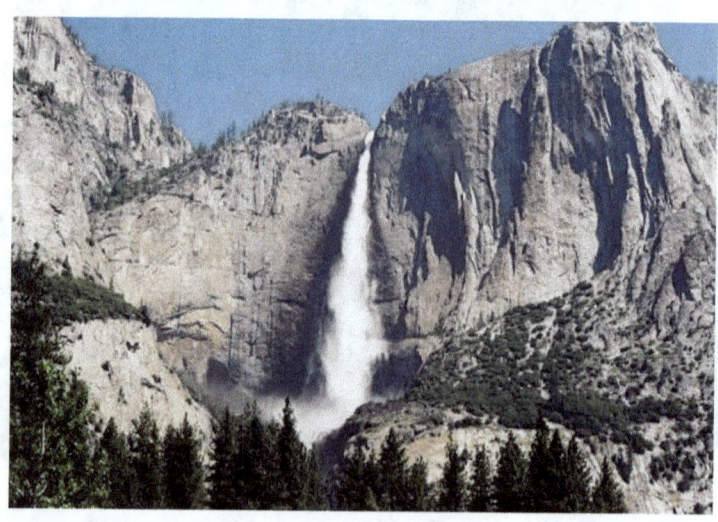

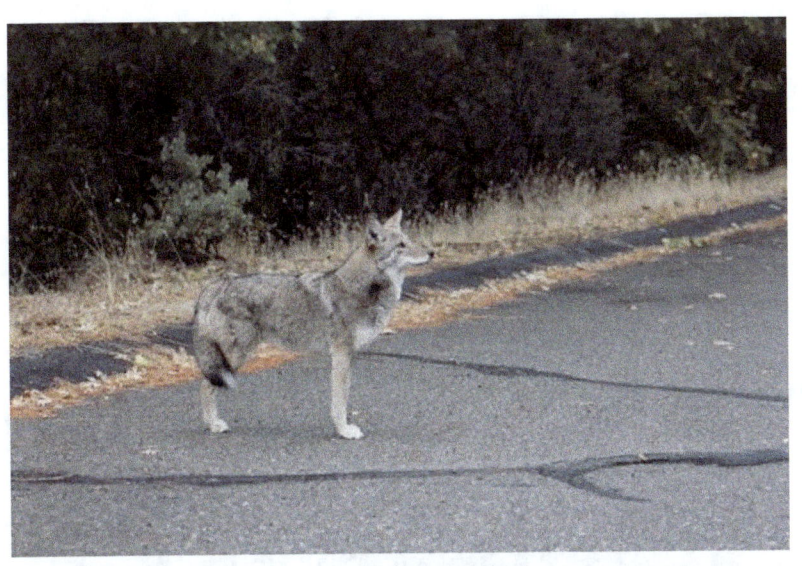

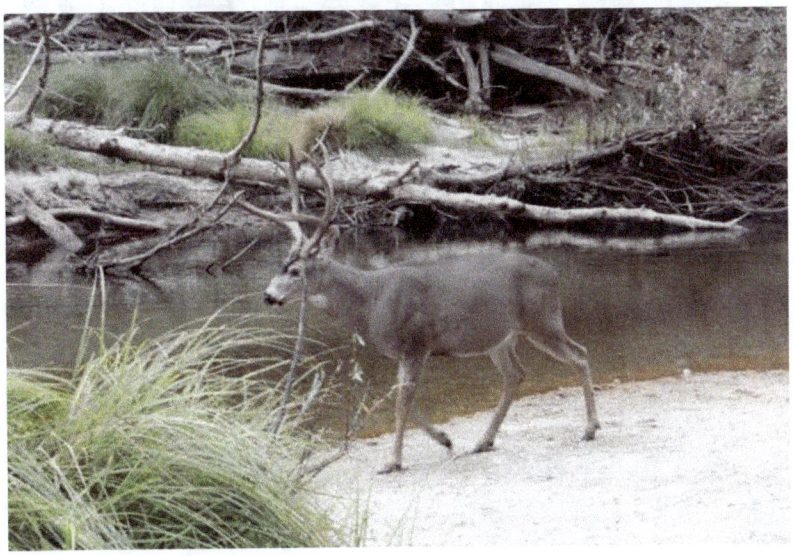

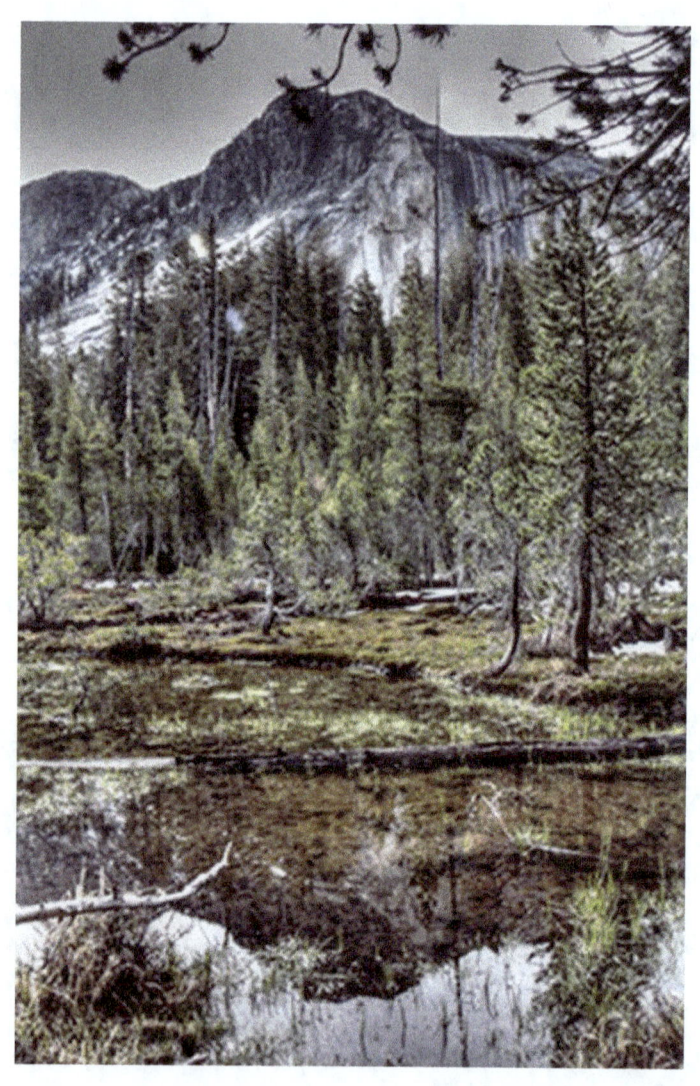

8. Sacramento Valley National Wildlife Refuge

The Sacramento Valley National Wildlife Refuge is located in the central valley and currently consists of over 70,000 acres. The complex consists of a group of several locations including wetlands, grasslands, and riparian habitats for a wide array of waterfowl, shorebirds, raptors, songbirds, waterbirds, reptiles, and mammals. The complex currently supports nearly 300 varieties of birds.

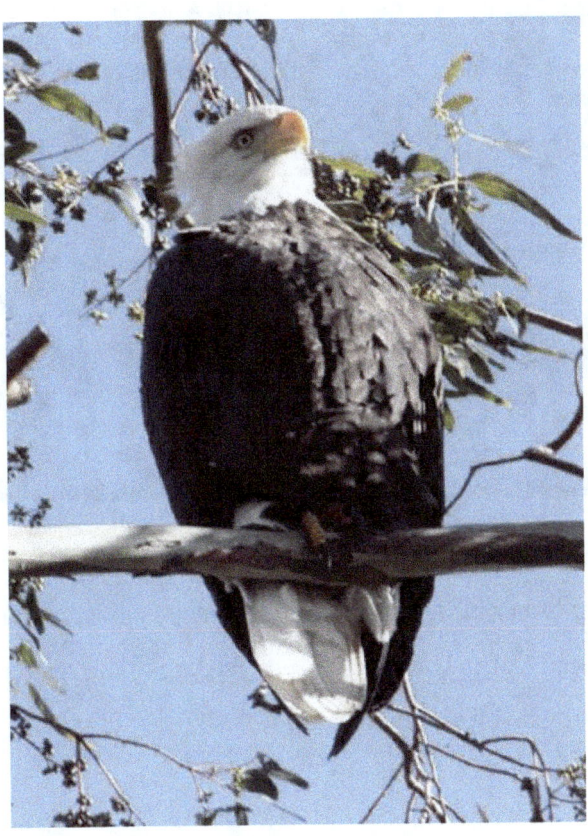

The Sacramento Valley National Wildlife Refuge is the winter stop for a large variety of migratory birds. The area is the winter home to Bald Eagles. Different areas of the refuge are home to specific types of birds. The Colusa Wildlife Refuge consists of over 5,077 acres and is the winter home of a large group of Night Herons. The Delevan Wildlife Refuge is mostly farmland and a stopover for Snow Geese.

The symbol of our nation, the Bald Eagle winters at the Sacramento Valley Wildlife Refuge along with a large number of Snow Geese and ducks.

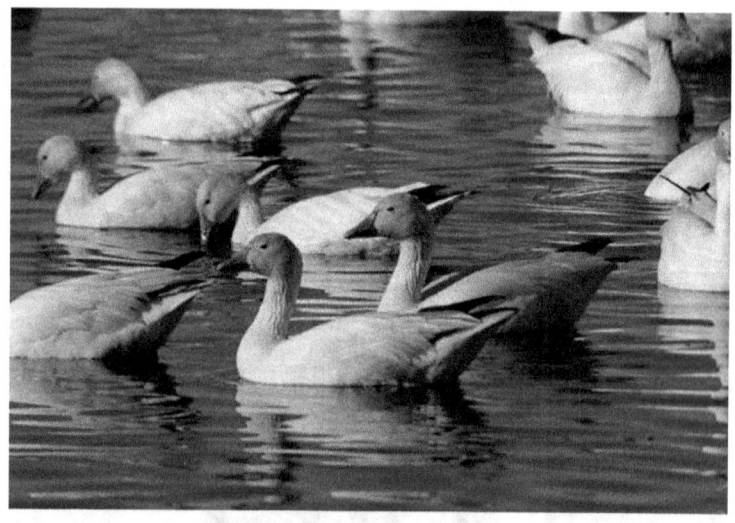

Snow Geese migrate to the refuge in early November by the thousands. Other birds that migrate to the area in large numbers are the American Coot. They can be seen feeding in the ponds that look like they are filled with cranberries.

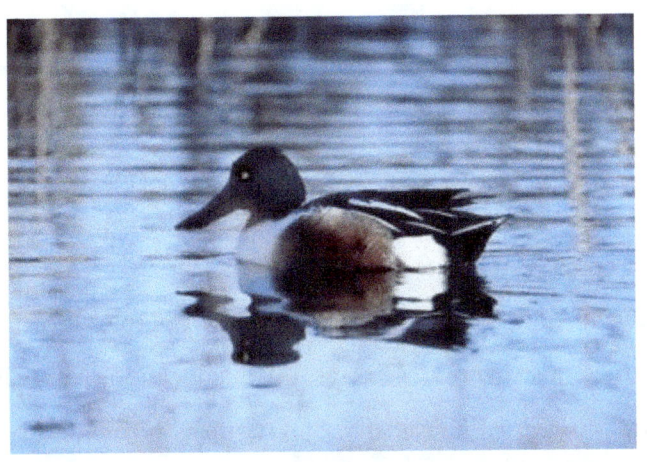

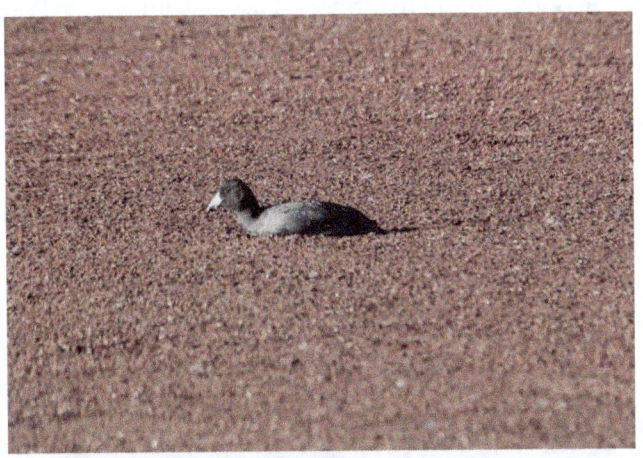

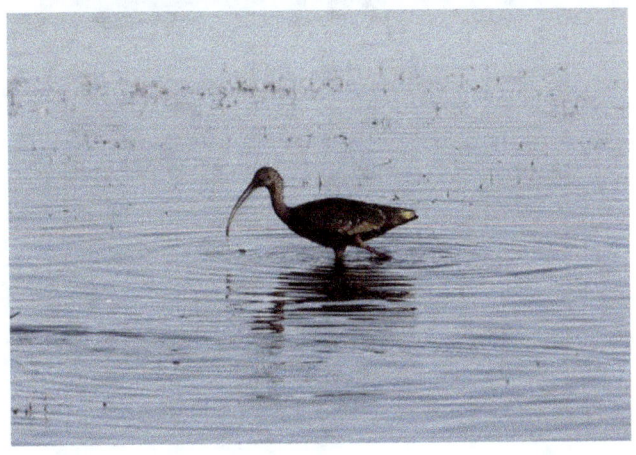

9. Colusa Wildlife Refuge

The Colusa Wildlife Refuge is east of Williams, California, located on Highway 20.

The refuge is one of six refuges located in northern California. It is a small refuge, just over 5,077 acres. At this location, you will find a large group of Ghost Herons (Night Herons), Shovelnose, Northern Ringneck, Coots (Mudhens), Snow Geese, Cinnamon Teal, Green Teal, hawks, deer, and turtles.

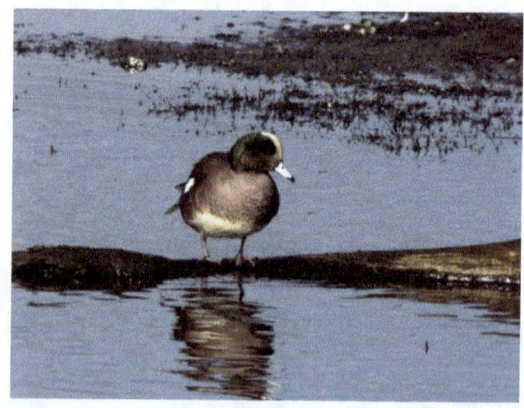

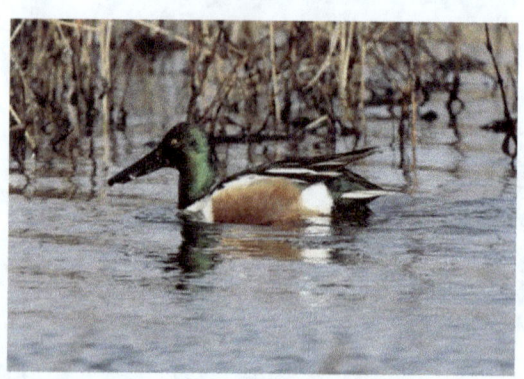

10. Lassen National Park

Reflection Lake is located at the north entrance to the park across from the Lake Manzanita Visitors Center. The center features a museum, outdoor theater, hiking trails, and beautiful vistas. A Great Blue Heron strolls the shore of Reflection Lake looking for food. Starting at Hat Lake at the base of Hat Mountain, the creek flows north to McArthur-Burney Falls and Lake Britton.

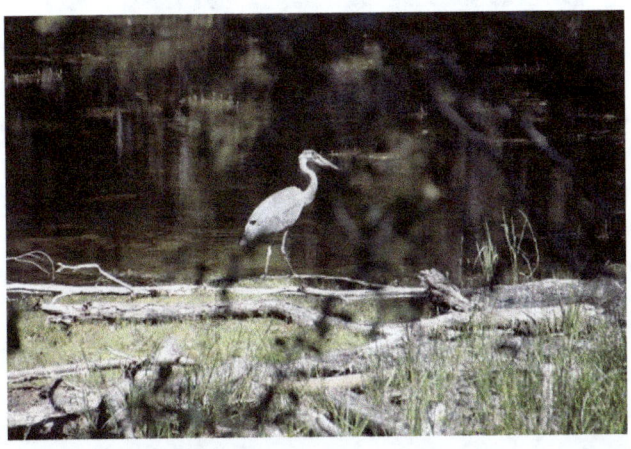

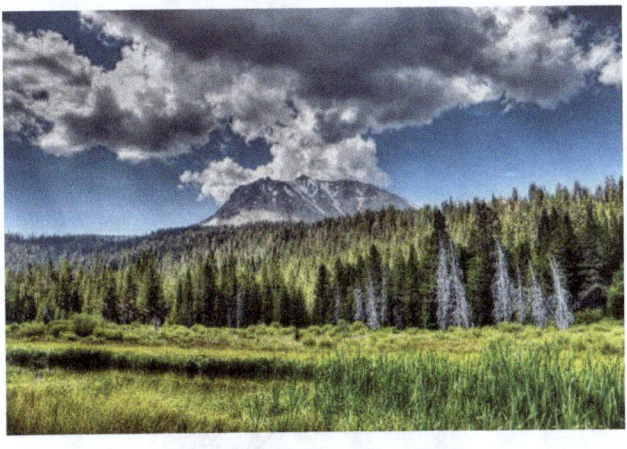

Kings' Creek flows through a meadow on its way to the Kings Creek Falls.

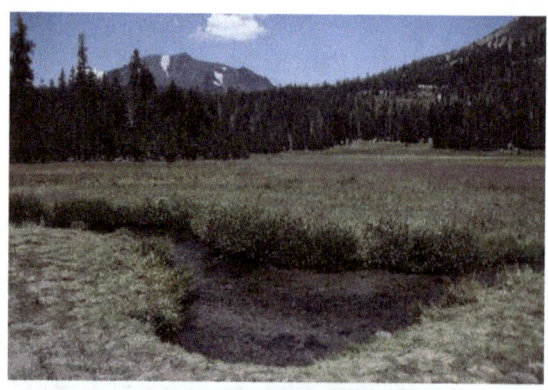

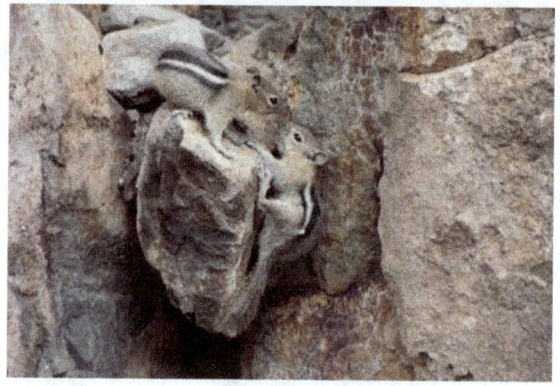

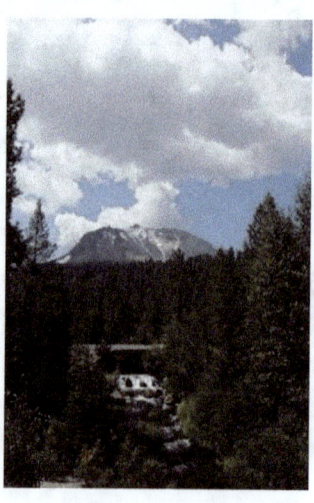

11. Hat Creek Area

Hat Creek begins at the base of Hat Mountain in Lassen National Park and flows north to Burney, California. It continues flowing over McArthur-Burney Falls and into Lake Britton.

This area is one of the top trout fishing areas in the state of California.

The McArthur-Burney Falls Memorial State Park center piece is the 129-foot Burney Falls. It is not only the tallest waterfall in the state park system but most likely the most beautiful.

The park area was created by volcanic activity and the falls are supplied by natural spring water which is snow melt collected in the layers of lava (basalt) creating large underground reservoirs. The water flow between the layers joins the waters of Hat Creek when it surfaces near Burney Falls. Because of the underground streams, one million gallons of water flow over Burney Falls every day. The park offers over five miles of hiking trails, including the Pacific Crest Trail and a trail to a historic cemetery with the gravesites of the family members who settled the area and preserved the area as a state park. Hiking the

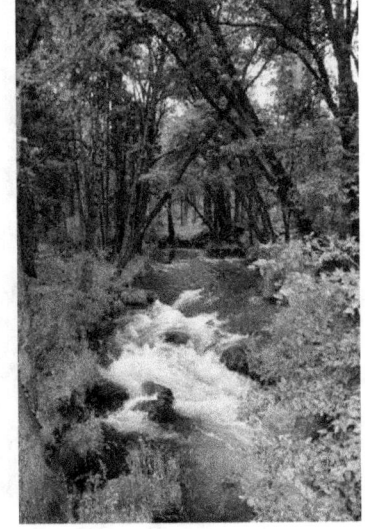

trails also offers a great opportunity to photograph many types of wildlife and flowers.

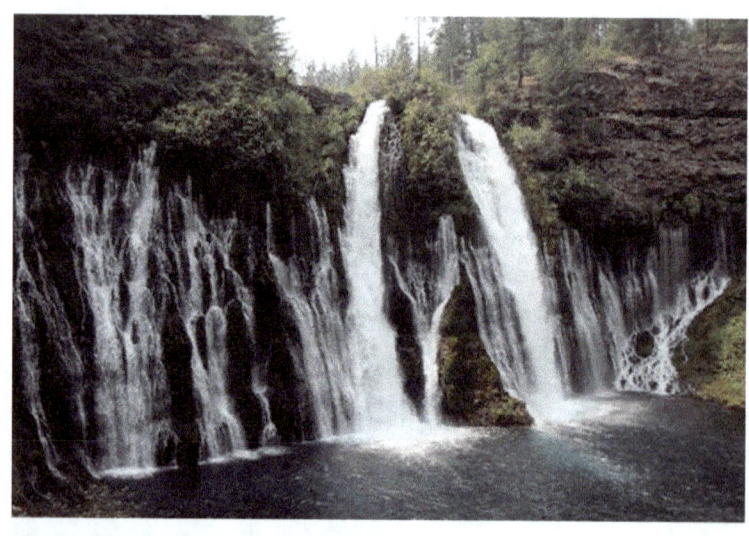

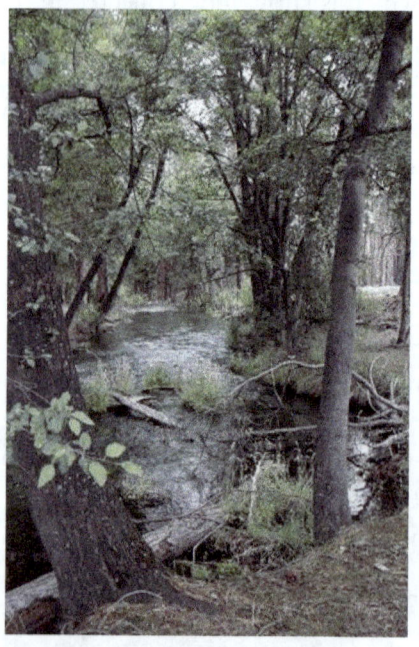

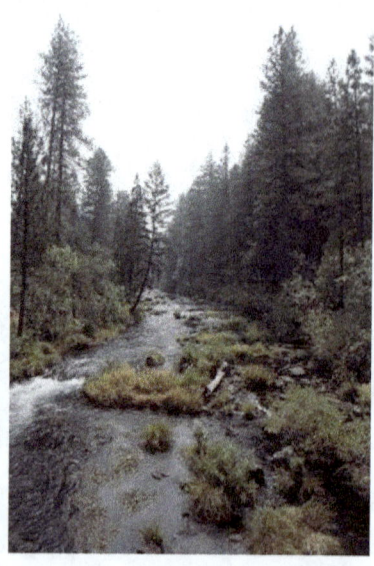

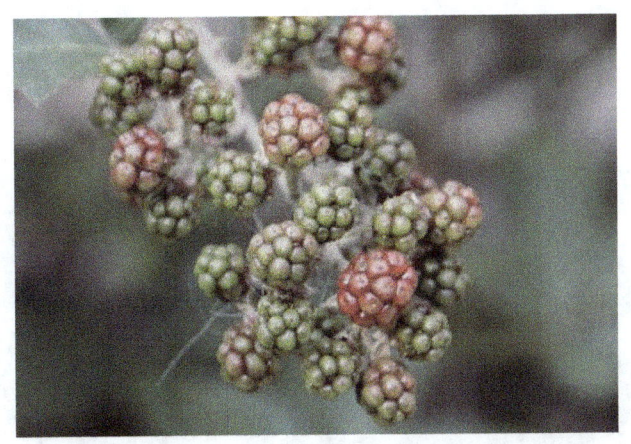

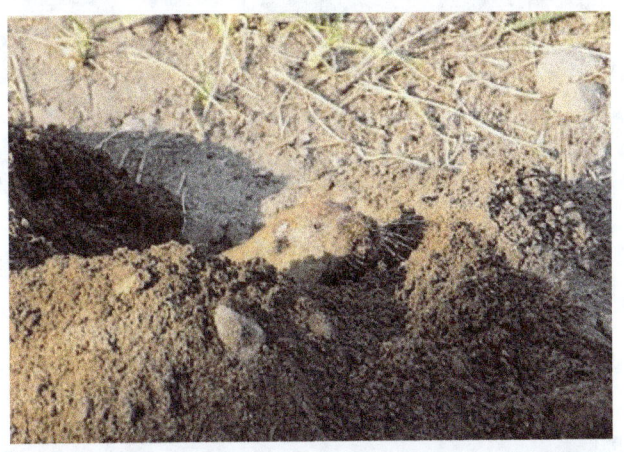

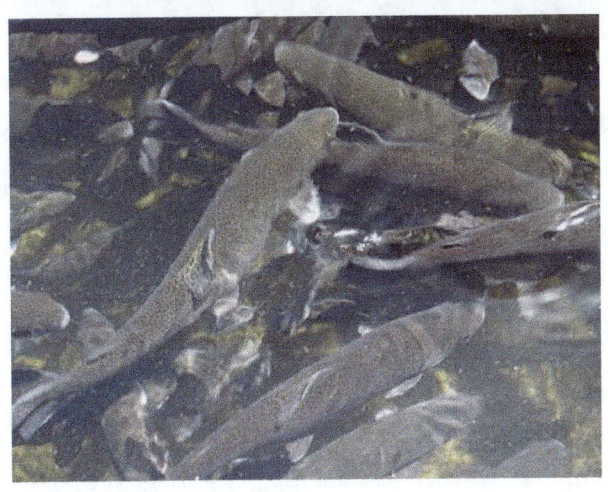

12. Pit River Area

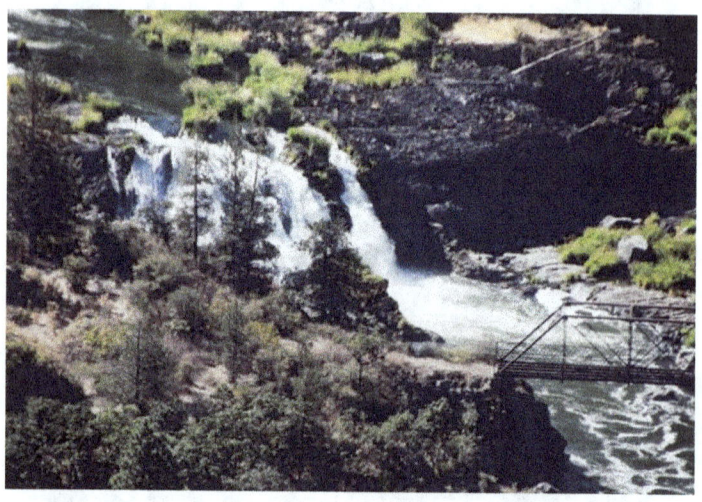

There is a beautiful view of the Pit River Falls from the Vista Point Parking area. The hike to the falls is long, hard, and hot in the summertime, but once you get there, the area is amazing for fishing and photography.

Thanks to AW (American Whitewater) for negotiating scheduled releases in October, this stretch has become an autumn classic, not to be missed. Foliage is beautiful. Water is clear and clean. Rapids are plentiful and you can run what might be the safest twenty-foot waterfall in the world.

Rapids on this run are caused by relatively recent volcanic activity. Especially at Big Eddy, lava flows have formed natural dams, which the river has incised to create unusual and sometimes spectacular rapids. At high flows there is a mandatory portage at Pit Falls, a thirty-foot vertical drop over a particularly large lava flow. At moderate flows such as the scheduled release, Pit Falls is a forty runnable class V, with a safe twenty-foot class IV waterfall on far right followed by a twenty-foot boat drag.

13. McCloud River

The McCloud River in Shasta County is a great recreational area. Locals use the river for camping, fishing, and swimming.

I enjoy the over three miles of trails, the wildflowers, wildlife, and the three waterfalls. The lower falls have become a local swimming hole in the summertime, where they have even installed a diving platform.

During the mid to late summer, the wildflowers bloom along the trail becoming home to a large variety of butterflies.

The middle falls are wide and slow moving compared to the lower falls. They remind me of the MacArthur-Burney Falls.

The upper falls are fast moving and flow through a narrow rocky gorge. The water jets out of the gorge and into a large pool below.

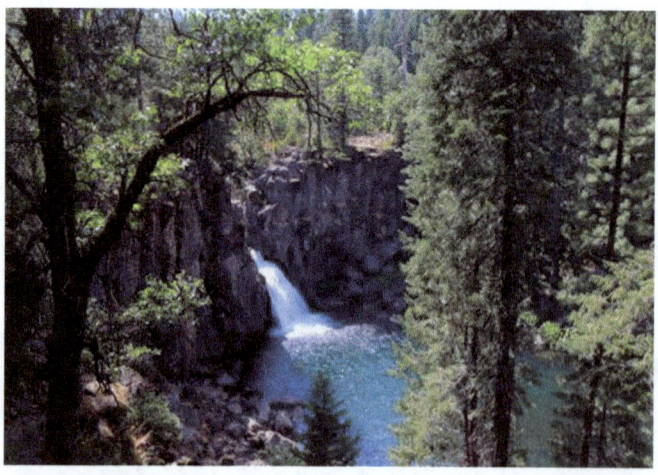

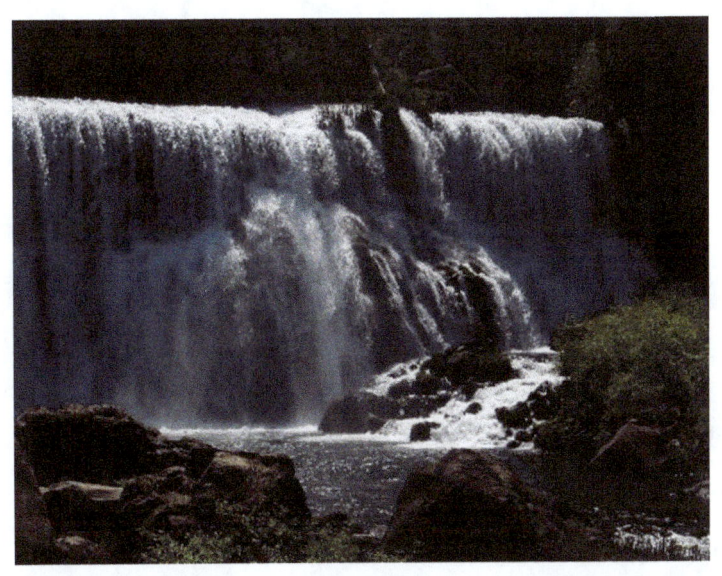

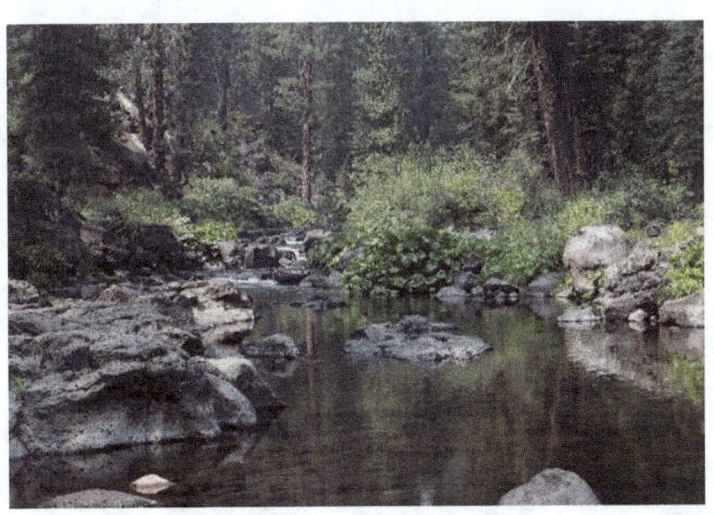

14. Dunsmuir Area

Mossbrae Falls

Mossbrae Falls is where the Sacramento River begins. The falls are about one hundred feet across and eight feet high. To get to the falls, you follow the Union Pacific railroad tracks north along the river for a mile until the tracks curve to the left. At that point, there is a trail to the falls on the right. This area is a great location for wildflowers, reptiles, and butterfly photography.

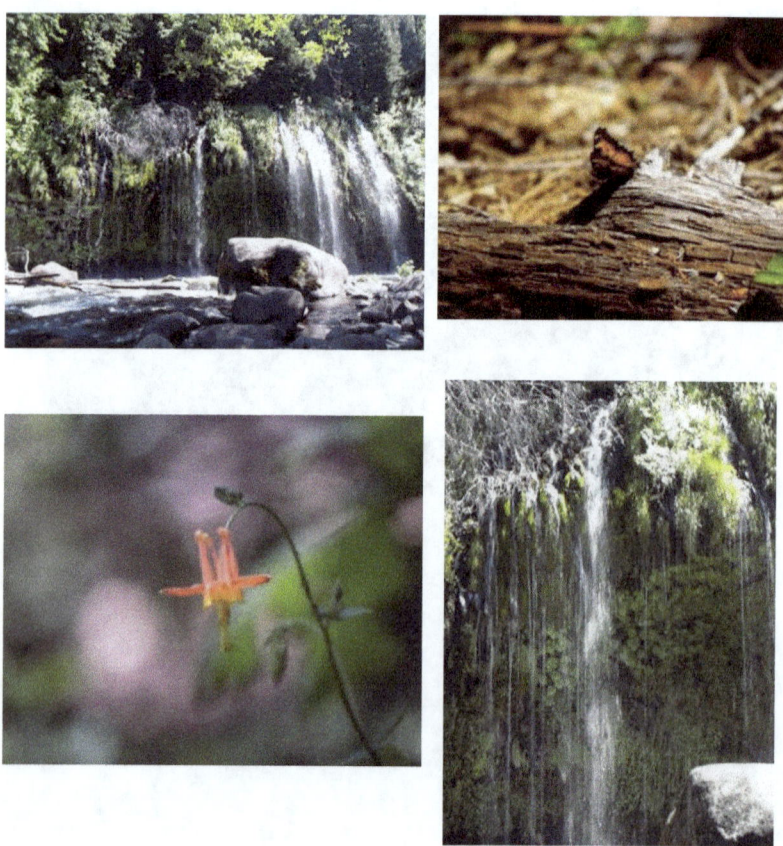

Hedge Creek Falls

The Falls are hidden in a public park on the north end of town. It took me years and many trips to find them. The locals kept telling me that it was in the town park. There are two parks in town, a large park along the Sacramento River and the smaller hidden park. To get to the falls you must park in a gravel area next to 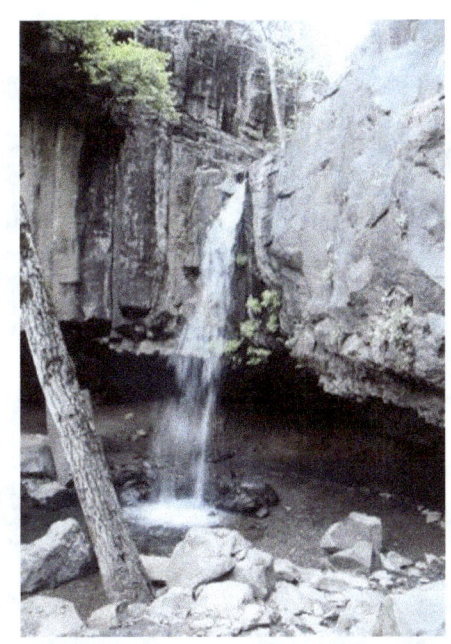 Interstate 5. Across the street, there is an overgrown area and behind it is the park. Once you enter the park through a small trail, you will see the grassy area and a gazebo. Follow the trail to the right and down into the canyon 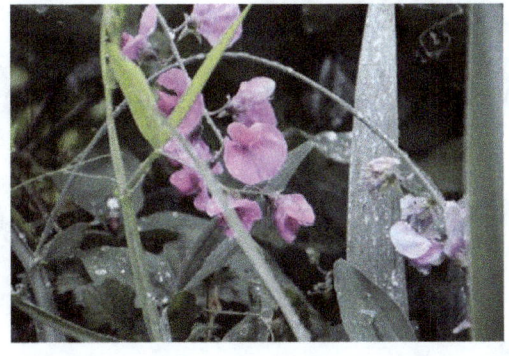 to the falls. The falls are a narrow stream of water falling about fifty feet. Over the years the water has eroded the ground and the trail continues behind the falls to the other side of the creek. Arrive early because children and adults come here to swim and meditate. This is another fantastic location for photographing birds, butterflies and bees on the plants and trees in the park. Sometimes you see things in nature that others do not!

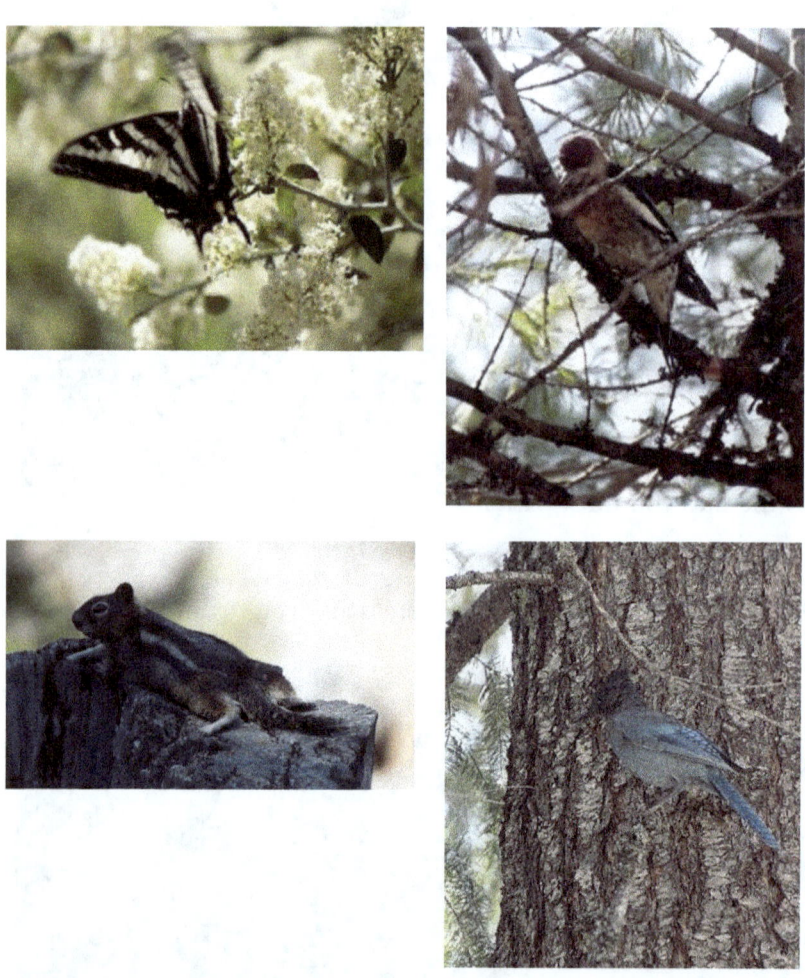

What do you see here?   Do you see what I saw?

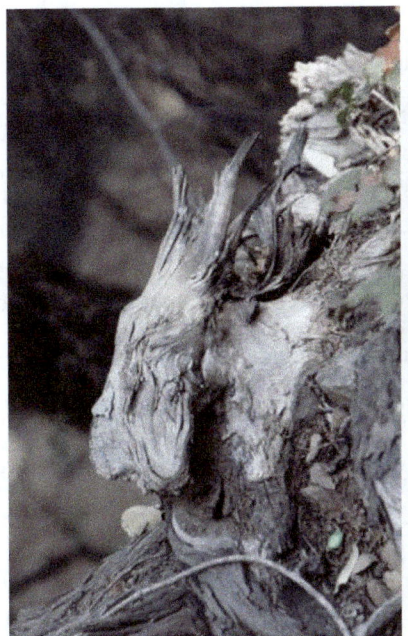 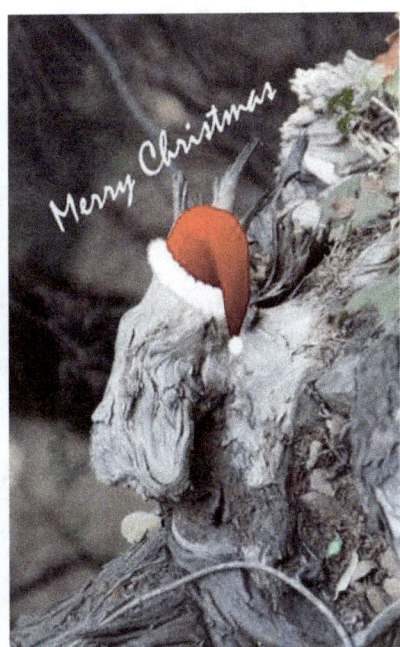

15. Point Reyes National Seashore

Point Reyes National seashore is located about an hour's drive north of San Francisco. Point Reyes National Seashore is over 70,000 acres and a preserve for the Tule Elk. Tomales Bay is the location where the San Andres Fault comes inland as it heads north to San Francisco.

The visitors center on Bear Valley Road is the location of the "Red Barn," home of the GSPS research facility. The barn contains seismology equipment monitoring the San Andres Fault. The fault line is marked by blue posts as it passes through the park. They are visible from the Earthquake Walk Trail. Also, along the trail you can see signs of the 1906 earthquake. Mounds rose up seventy feet along the fault, and a fence separated twenty feet during the shifting of the fault.

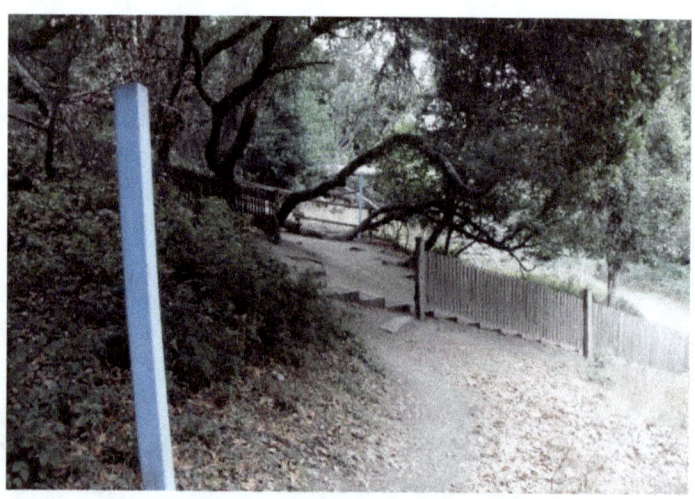

There is an abundance of wildlife in the park, including elk, deer, fox hawks, falcons, bobcats, mountain lions, reptiles, migratory birds of all types, squirrels, and a breeding ground for Elephant Seals.

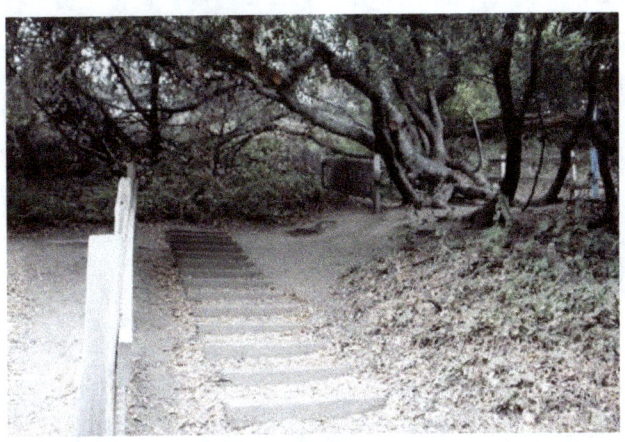

The north part of the park is the Pierce Point Ranch at the entrance to the Tule Elk Preserve. Migratory birds can be found at many locations. Two of my favorite locations are Lamitore Beach and Abbott Lagoon.

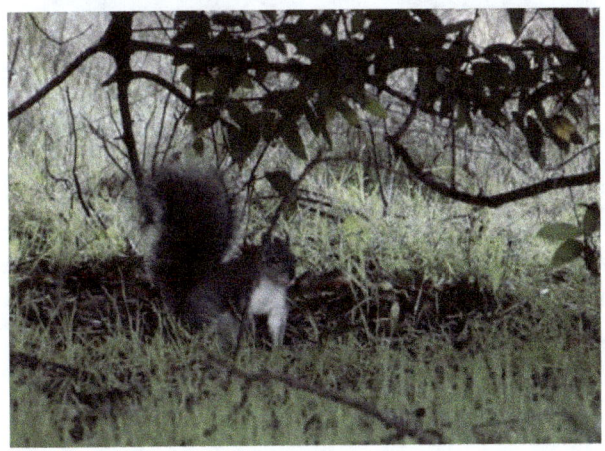

Gray Squirrel

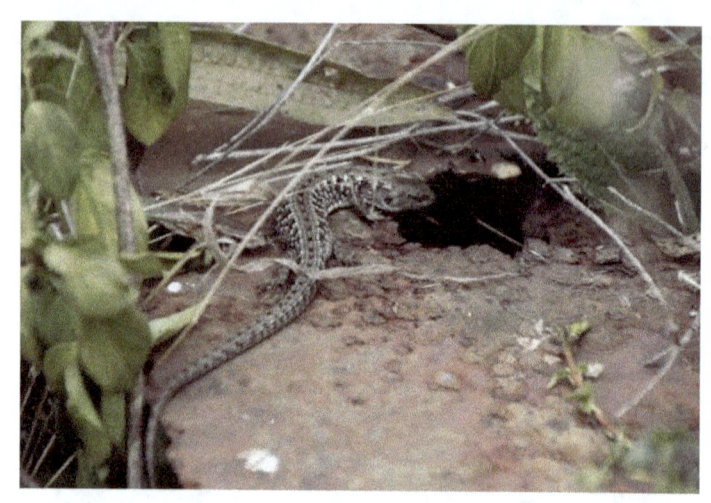

Alligator Lizard

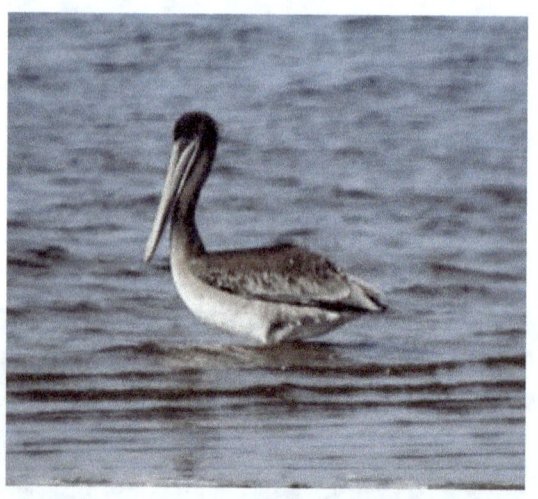

Brown Pelican

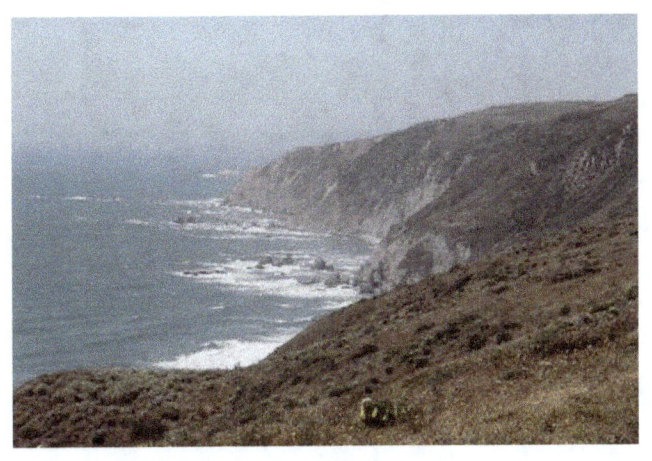

North Coastline of Point Reyes

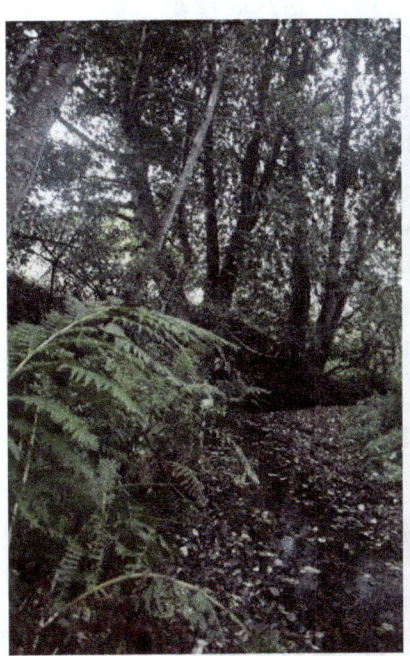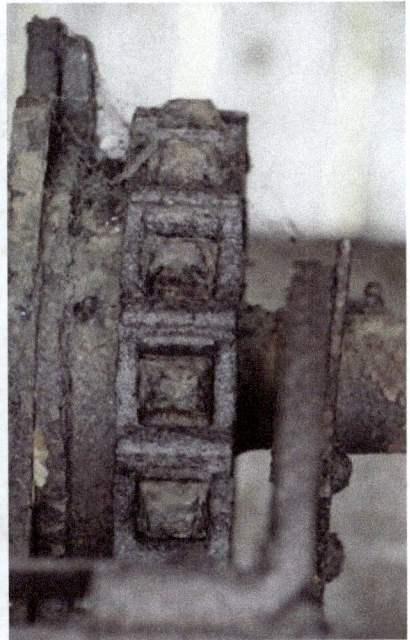

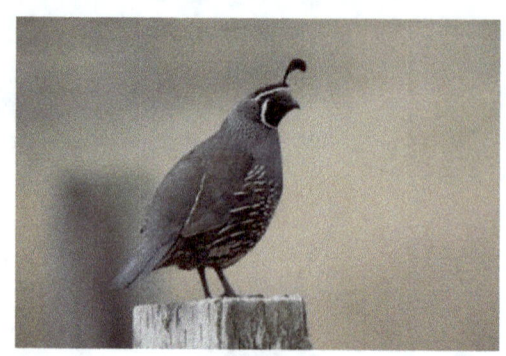

California Quail

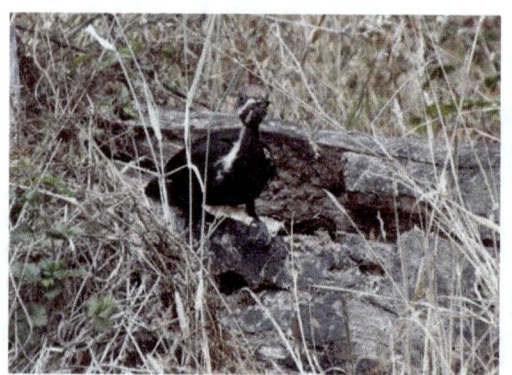

Woodpecker

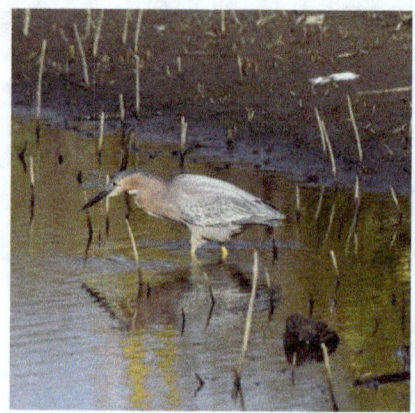

Green Heron

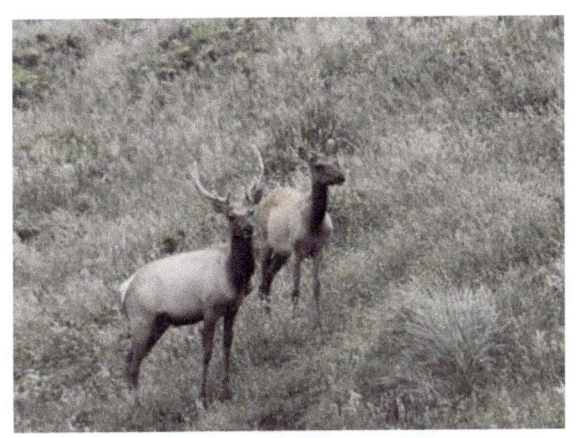

Tule Elk

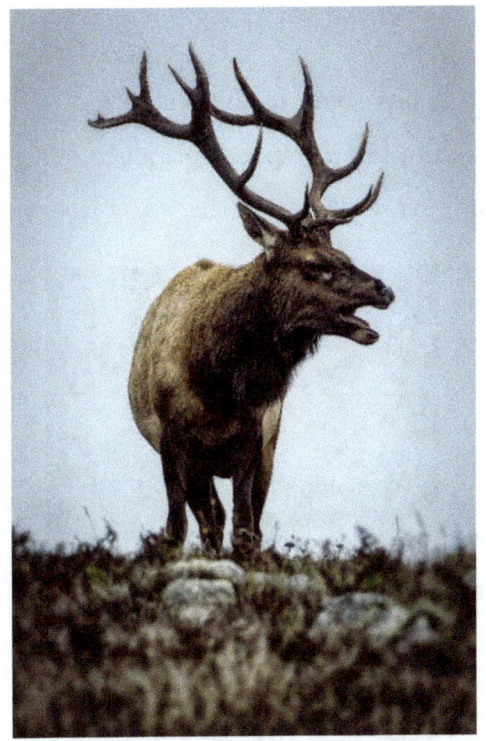

Bull Elk

16. Muir Woods National Monument

Muir Woods National Monument is approximately a 30-minute drive north of San Francisco. In 1905, Congressman William Kent and his wife, Elizabeth Thacher Kent, purchased 611 acres to protect the giant redwoods and donated 295 acres to the federal government. In 1908, President Theodore Roosevelt declared it a national monument. The President wanted to name it after William Kent, but William Kent insisted that it should be named after conservationist John Muir.

Muir Woods contains some of the oldest and tallest trees in the world. The park is a photographer's paradise. The giant redwoods, streams, wildlife, and wildflowers make a visit well worth it.

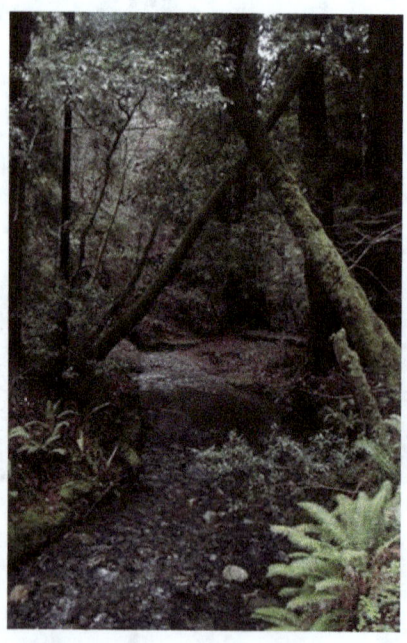

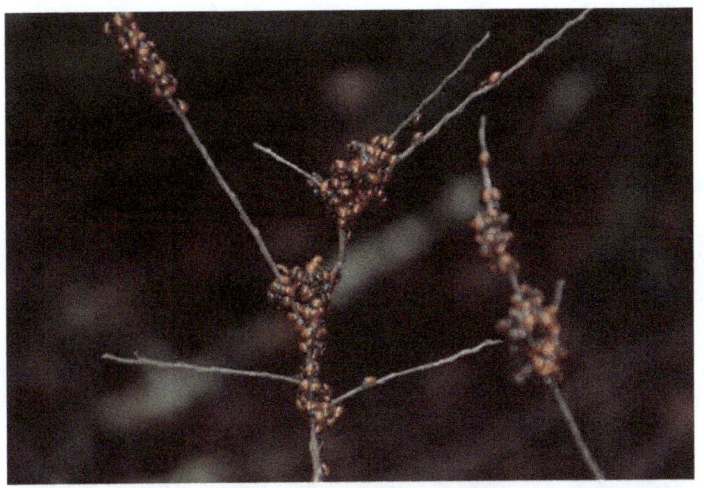

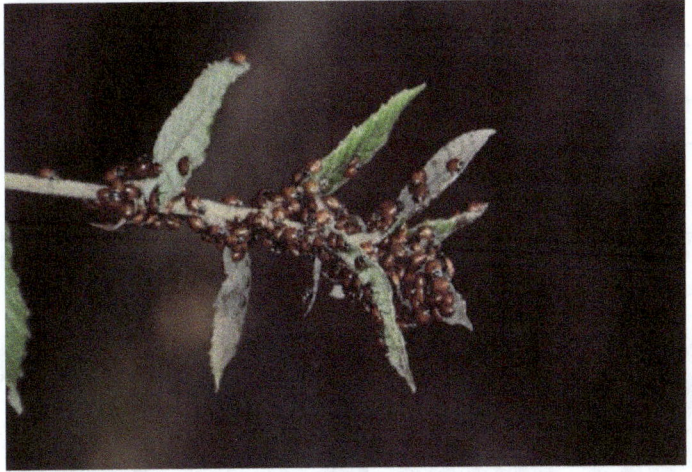

In the middle of February, the lady bugs come out of hibernation and begin to swarm. During this time of the year, you can find thousands of them on the ground, plants, and trees. After a week, they leave and spread throughout California.

17. Santa Cruz Area

Santa Cruz, California, is famous for its Beach & Boardwalk and lesser known for Natural Bridges State Park with its Monarch Butterfly Preserve and the UC Santa Cruz Arboretum Hummingbird Trail.

Natural Bridges State Park

Natural Bridges State Park is named for the arch formations created by waves along the shoreline and lesser known for the thousands of Monarch butterflies that winter there. You can also find a large variety of wildlife, beautiful views of the coastline, and several other types of butterflies.

Monarch Chrysalis (Left)   Monarch Caterpillars (Right)

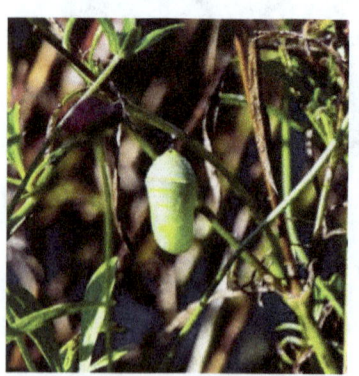 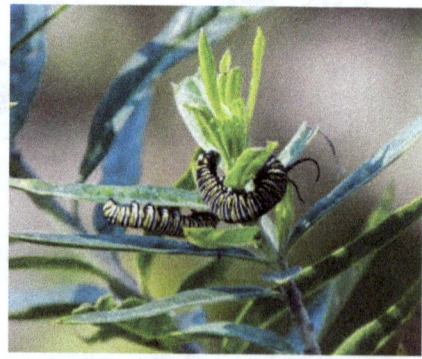

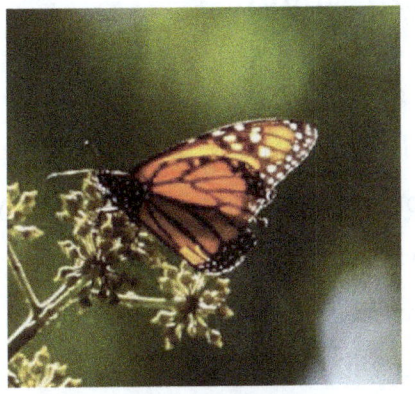

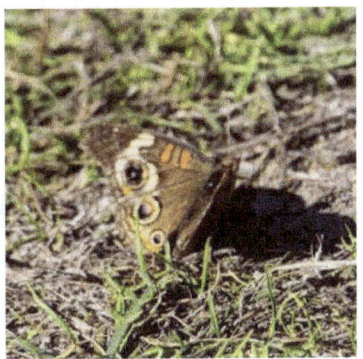

Buckeye

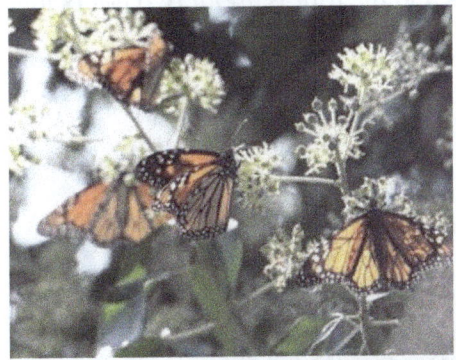

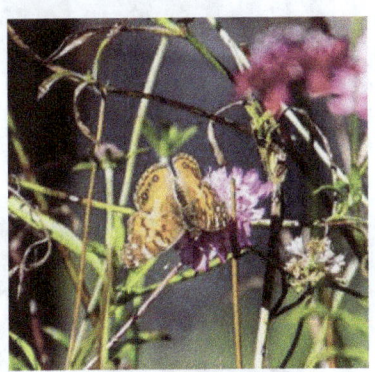

Painted Lady

18. Elkhorn Slough

The Elkhorn Slough near Moss Landing is home to a large group of sea otters. The Elkhorn Slough Safari is the only company allowed by the California Department of Fish and Game to use a boat to come with fifteen feet of the sea otters. When I visit the slough, I hire a pontoon boat tour with the Elkhorn Slough Safari for twenty-two photographers and the tour is about two hours long. During the tour you will see Harbor Seals, pelicans, herons, cormorants, and sometimes several large groups of sea otters called "Rafts." (Below)

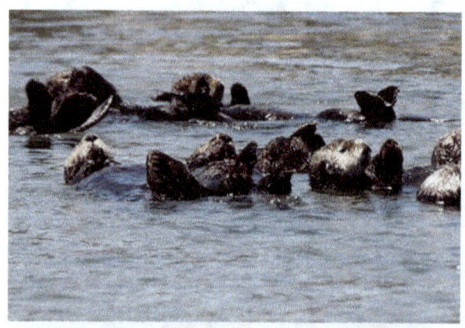

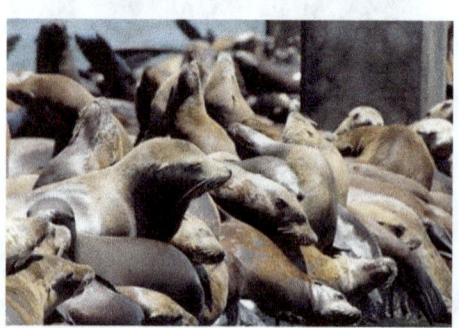

Harbor Seals

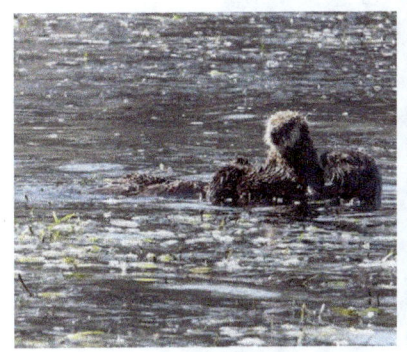
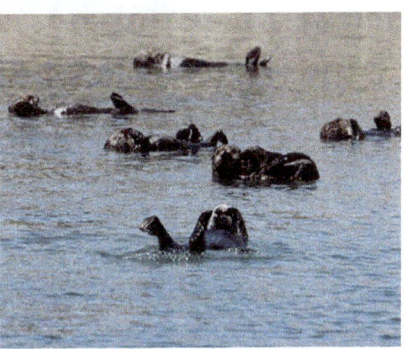

Mom with Pup

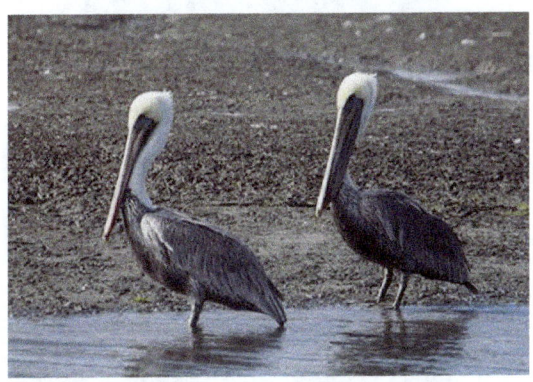

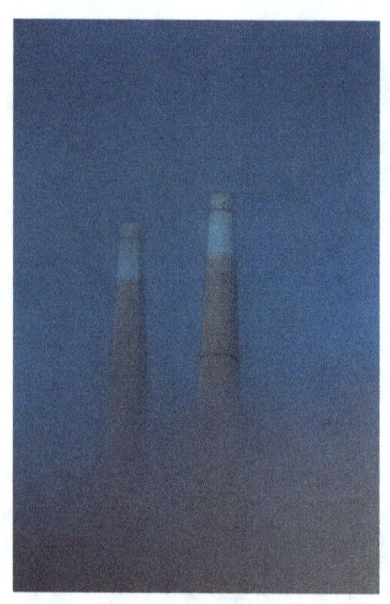

Moss Landing Towers

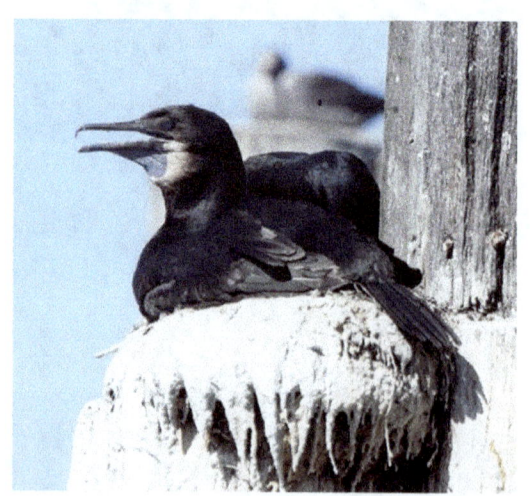

Cormorant

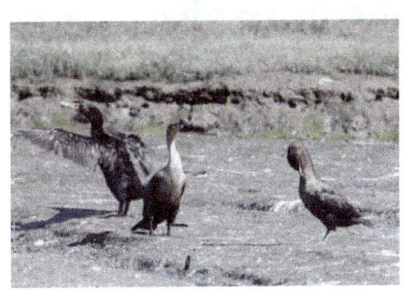 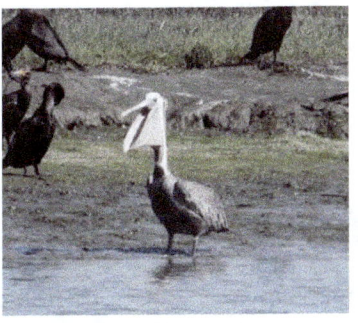

This way, follow me!   I'm on my way!

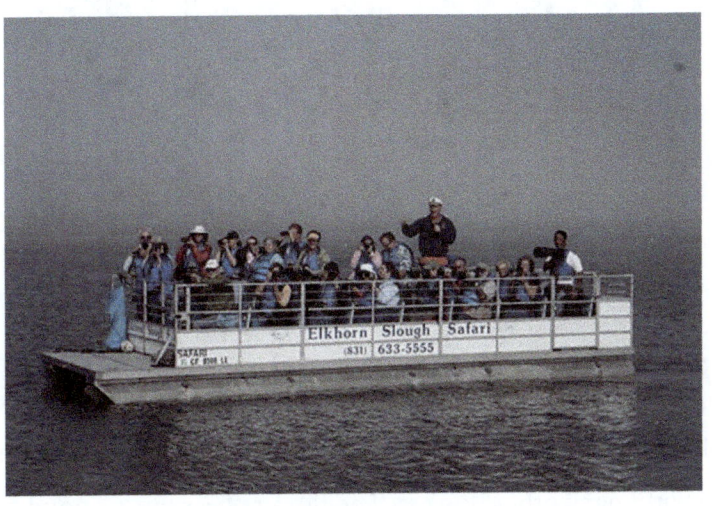

Elkhorn Slough Safari

19. Hallberg Butterfly Garden

The Hallberg Butterfly Garden located in Sonoma County is home to a beautiful garden with ponds and a variety of trails on nine acres tucked away in an apple orchard. Louise Hallberg would greet each visitor every day and would explain the history of the garden.

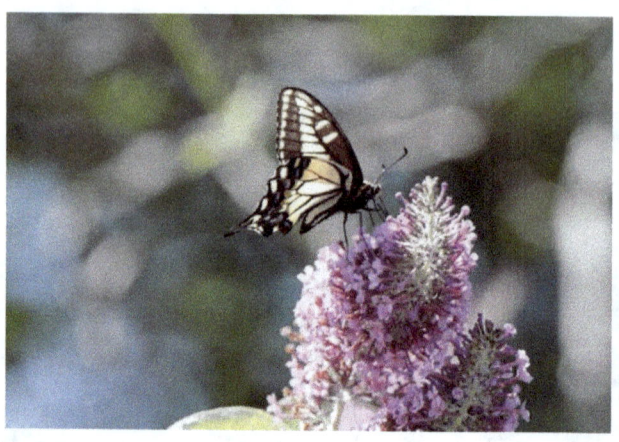

The garden is home to a variety of butterflies, including the Pipevine Swallowtail, the star of the garden. Pinevine grows wild in the garden along with many other flowers. The flowers near the lily pond attract several types of bees, dragonflies, and mayflies that fill the sky. Quail, fox, blue jays, robins, several types of black birds, hummingbirds, and even wild turkey have been seen roaming the orchard.

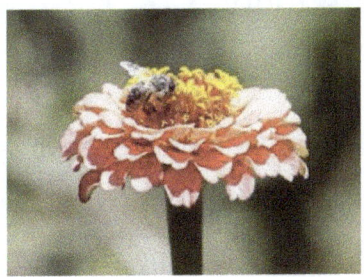 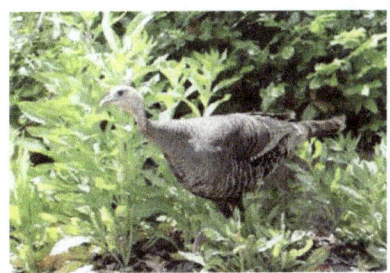

The main attraction at the Hallberg Butterfly Garden is the Pipevine Swallowtails

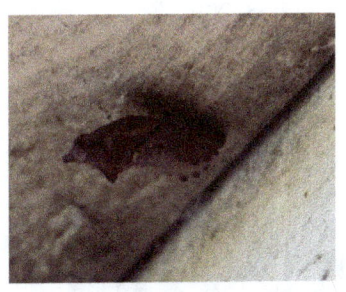 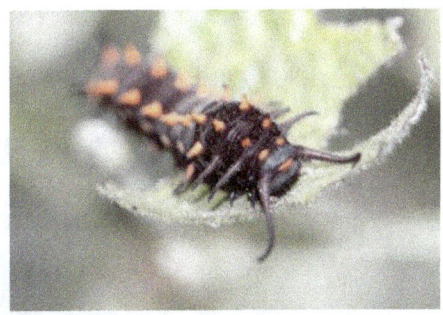

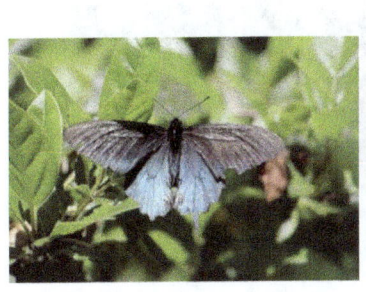 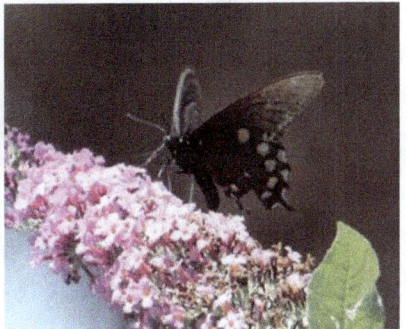

20 Ironstone Winery

Ironstone Winery, Murphys, California, is a great springtime trip up Highway 4 into the Gold Country. There are plenty of landscape and wildlife photography opportunities, good food, and don't forget the wine! Ironstone has a summer concert series with major recording artists. Also, they have an onsite gold mine and museum, flower garden and gift shop. Some of the best features of the winery are the flower gardens and the historic mining equipment on site. The museum even has a large gold nugget in a glass vault.

The tulips, daffodils, and vineyards make great photo opts.

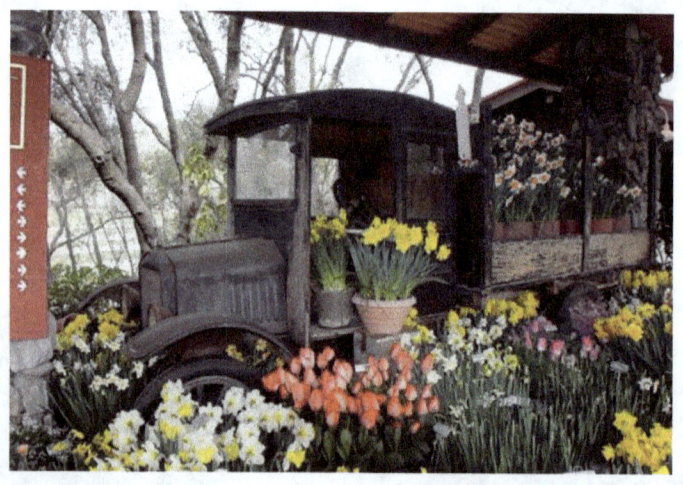

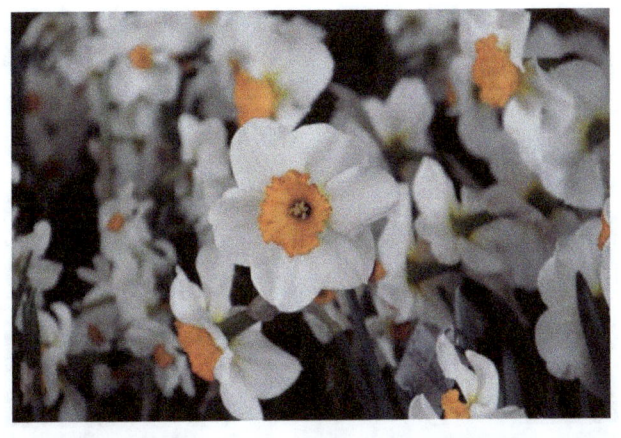
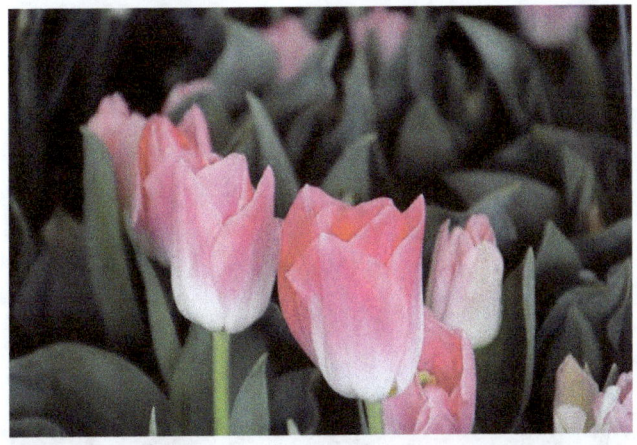
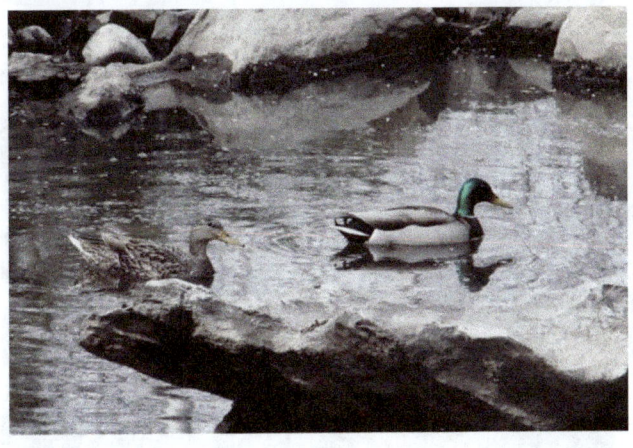

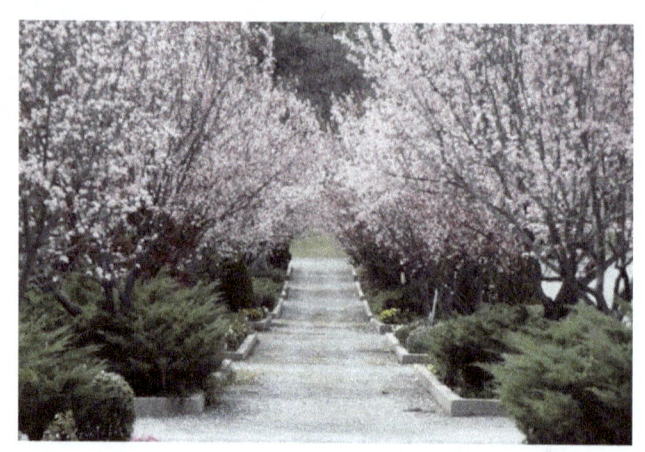

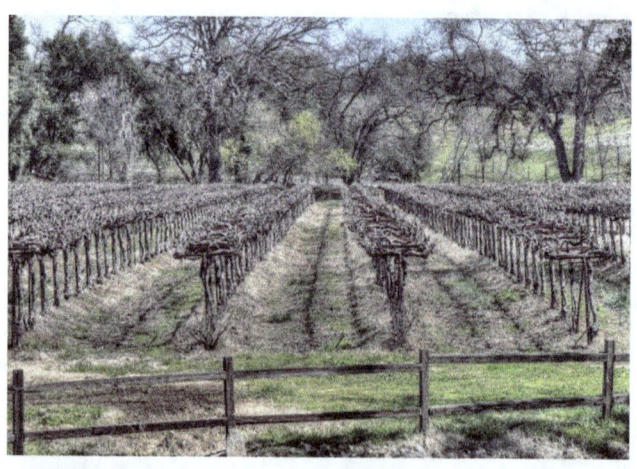

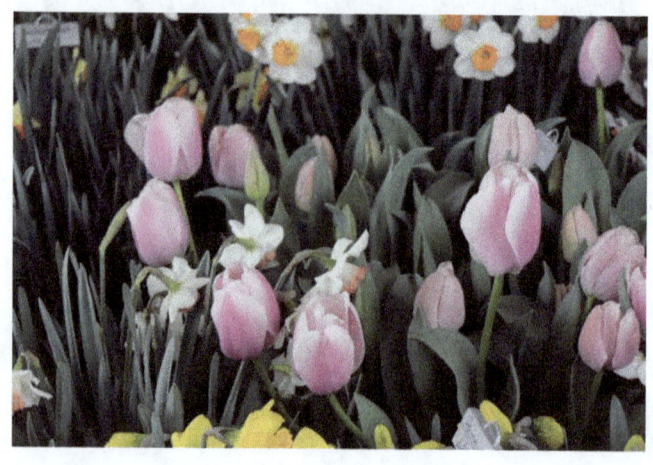

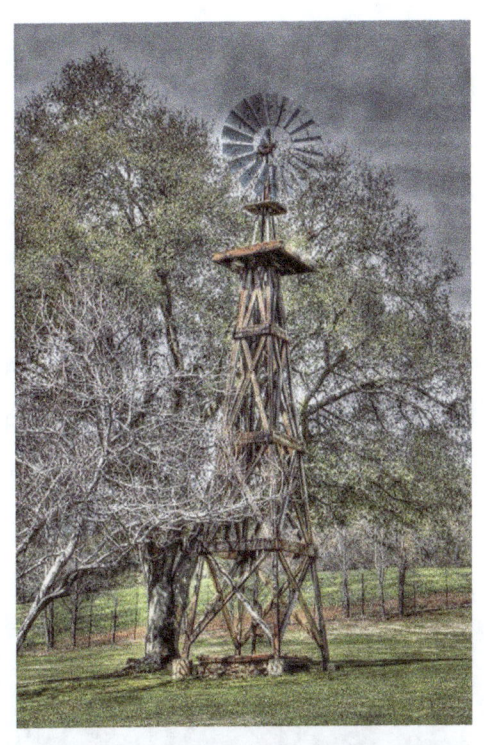

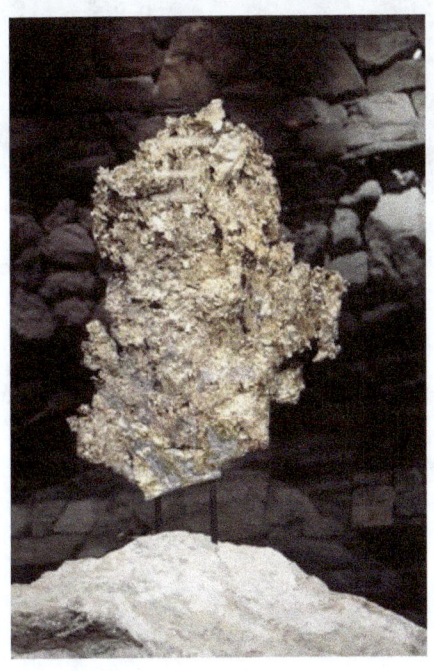

21. Uvas Canyon Regional Park

Uvas Canyon County Park just outside of Gilroy, California, is a beautiful park filled with green ferns, wildflowers, grasslands, oak trees, streams, waterfalls, wildlife, and ladybugs. If you've been to Muir Woods and like ladybugs, then Uvas Canyon is a place you will love. In early March, the ladybugs come out of hibernation and begin to swarm. Millions of the small red and black bugs can be seen everywhere.

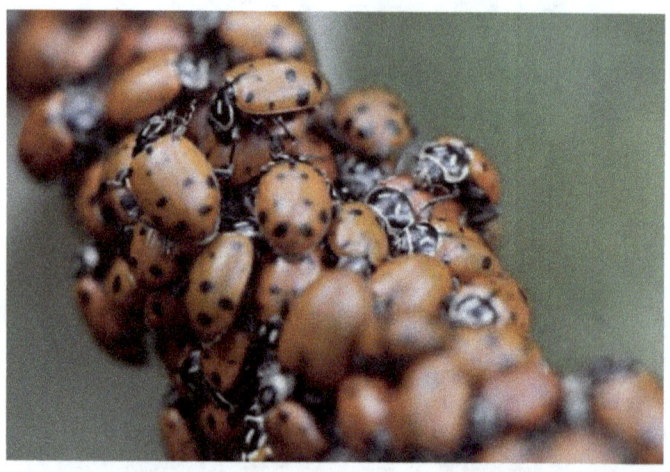

Every year I lead my Meetup.com Wildlife & Landscape Photography group to Uvas Canyon. The event is called "Ladybugs & Waterfalls."

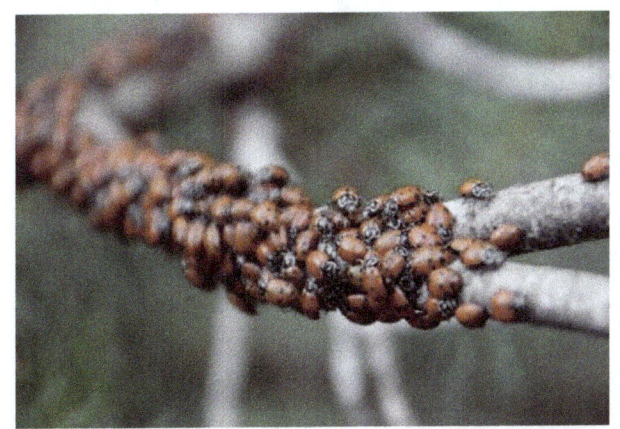

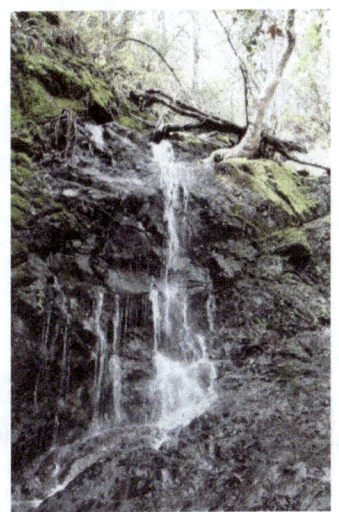 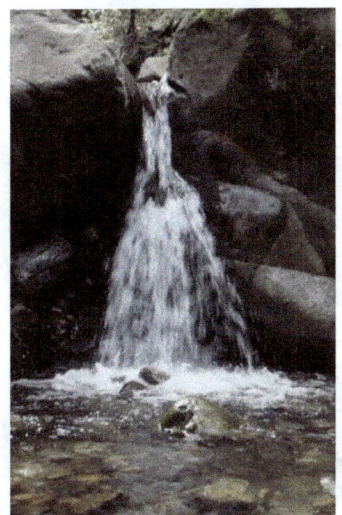

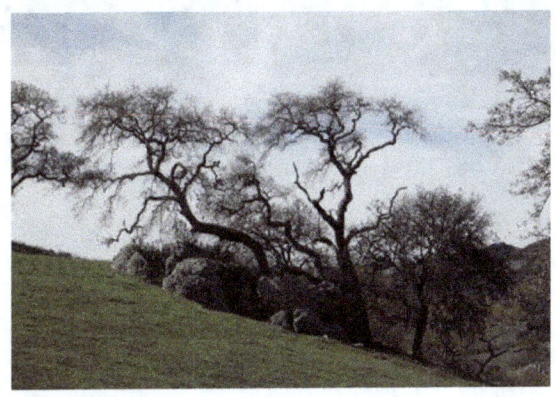

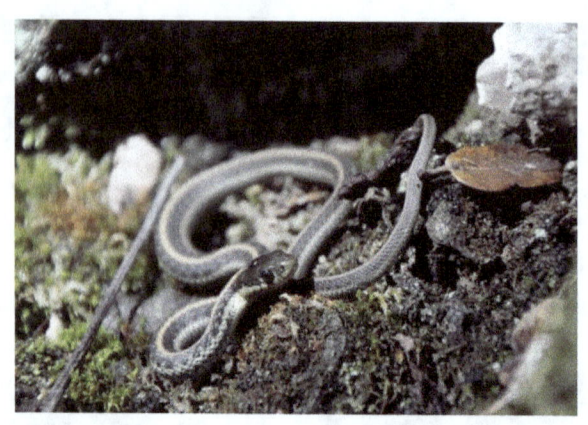
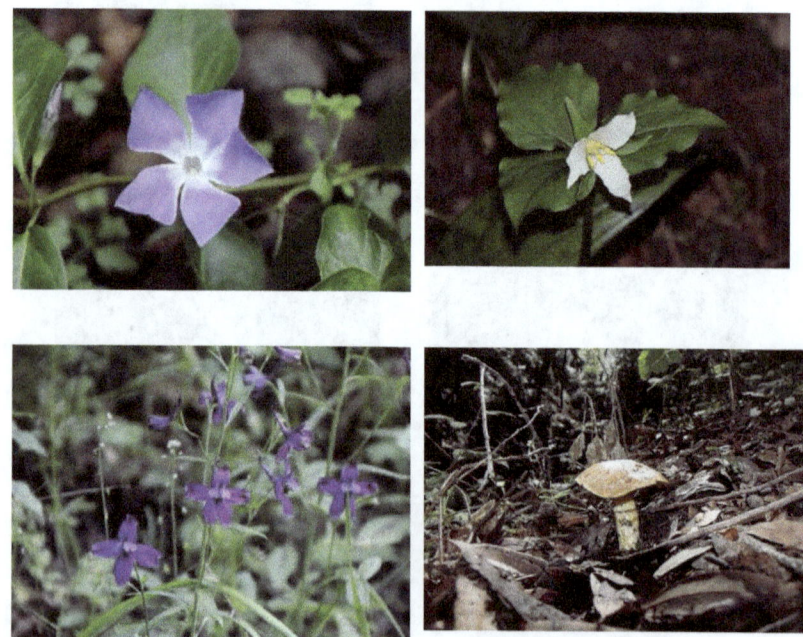

22. Carson Pass Area

The Carson Pass area offers a large variety of photography opportunities. The area has large granite formations, several lakes, streams, waterfalls, barns, meadows with wildflowers, and abandoned cabins. The vistas are breathtaking! It is such a large area that you cannot see it all in one day.

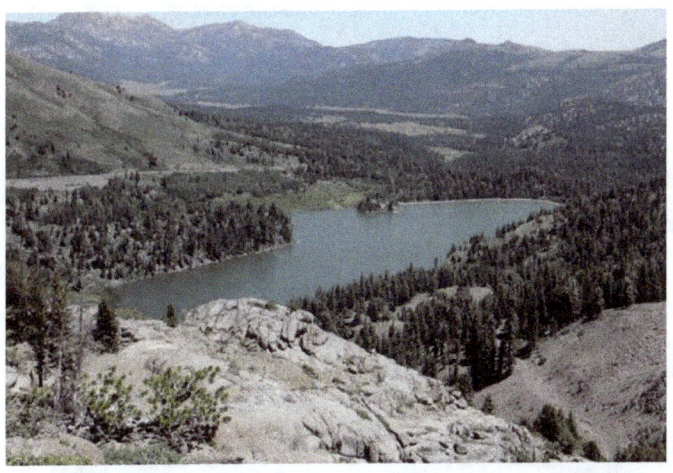

The trailhead at the Carson Pass Visitors Center takes you to Frog Lake and Lake Winnemucca. From Frog Lake, the amazing views of the large granite formations like Elephant Back, Red Lake Peak, and Round Top Peak make you feel small in a large world.

There is a small campground at Kirkwood Lake. When you hike through the campground to the stream north of the Kirkwood Lake, you arrive at Kirkwood Falls. The water cascades over the granite formation until it gets to the falls that drops thirty feet and continues cascading down the mountain into a valley.

Woods Lake is a small lake with several campgrounds and a small but tall cascading waterfall that flows from a large meadow near The Lost Gold Mine.

The famous fall colors of Hope Valley and the cabin (below) are a perfect scenery for a landscape photographer.

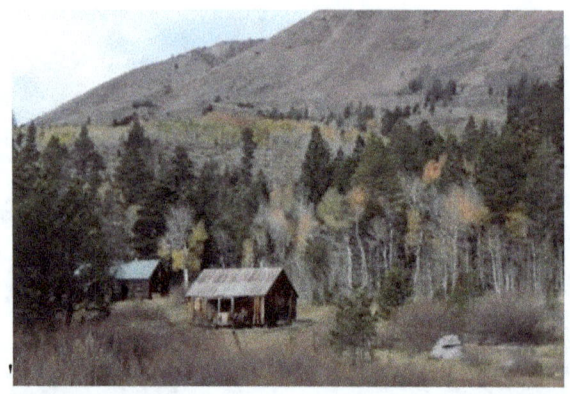

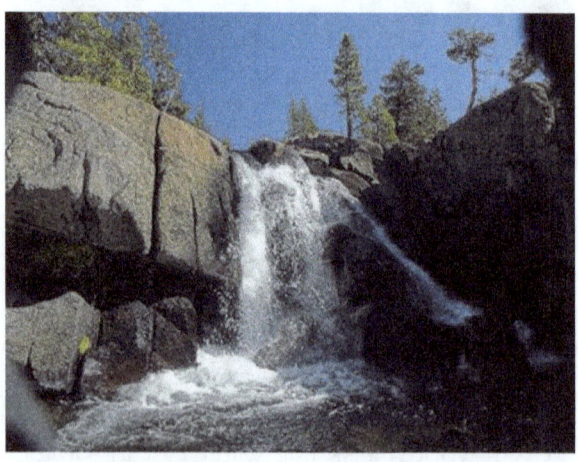

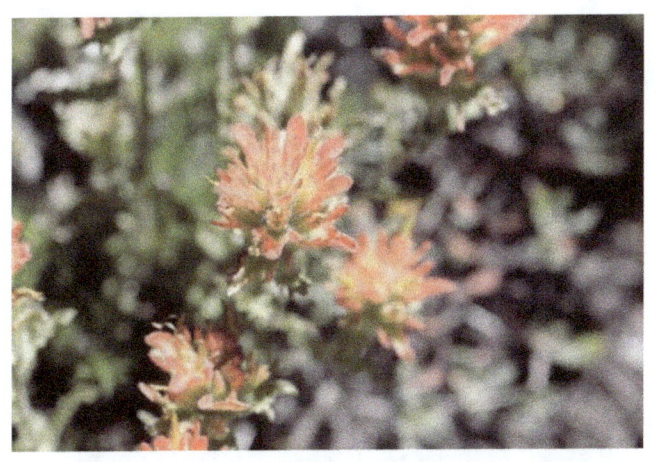

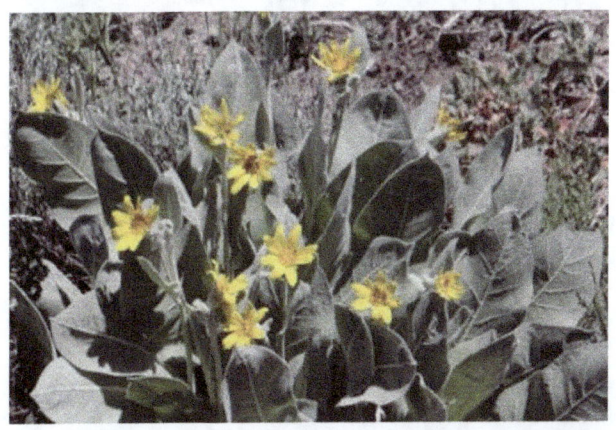

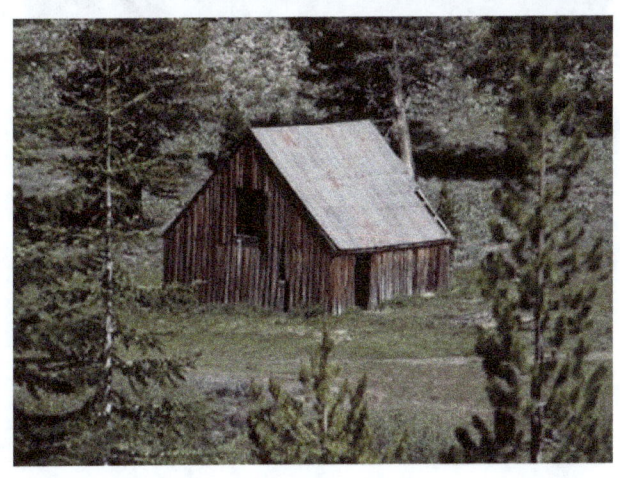

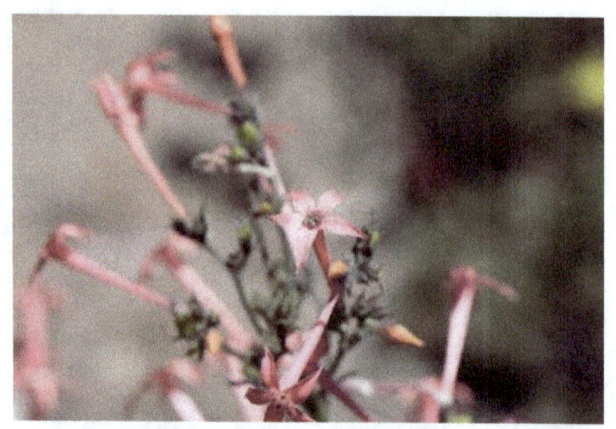

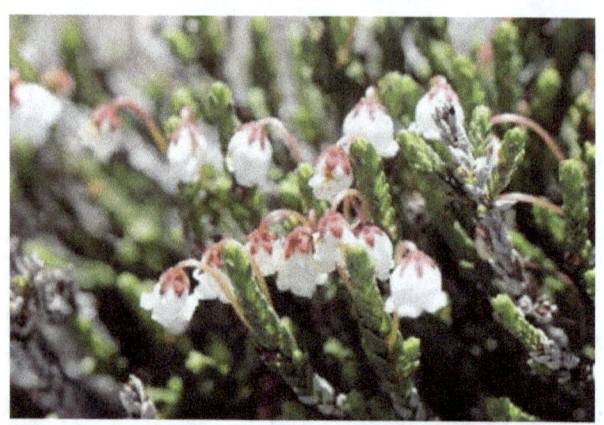

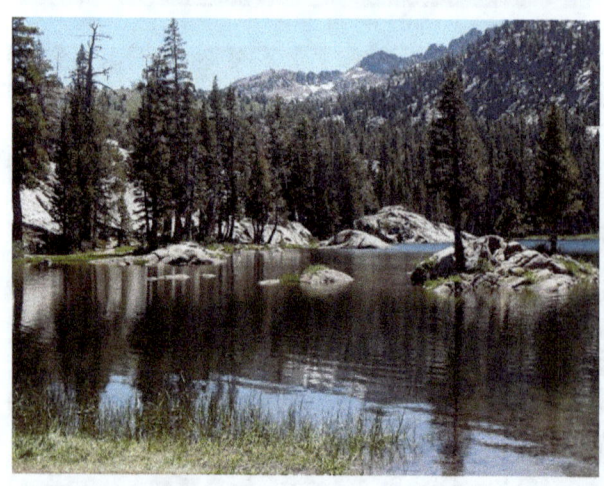

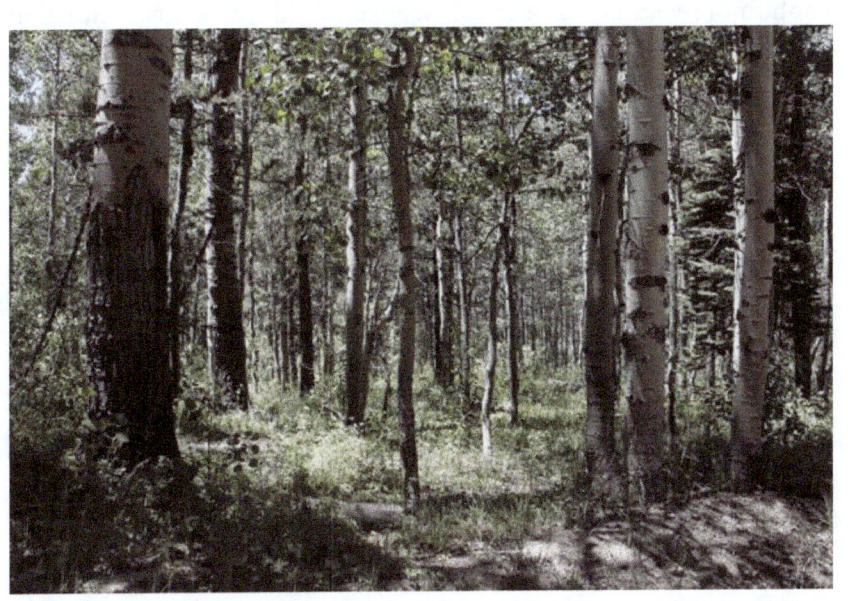

About the Author

Photographing California is a great pastime of mine. On day trips, I visit locations throughout California and record them with my camera for friends and family.

I was introduced to photography while in a biology class during my sophomore year in high school. We were told by the instructor that he was going to teach us how to make slides for the microscope and photograph the slides. We were in a new school with extra rooms and the other high school across town had unused darkroom equipment. Our biology teacher and a group of students constructed eight darkrooms in an empty room next to the lab.

I was sold on photography; I spent the entire year photographing anything that did not move. I developed the film and printed everything in black and white. During the summer, the instructor loaned me the equipment I needed and gave me chemicals and paper that would have expired if they were not used.

I later setup my own darkroom and began to work with color images. Today I travel the western states and have my own digital darkroom.

About the Book

The book describes areas that I have visited and photographed over the years. These are areas that I return to repeatedly and would like to share them with you. Each chapter is about a specific area. Some chapters may consist of several areas near each other. Some chapters may also be about areas that will require at least half a day of travel time from the Bay area. I recommend that you plan on staying several days, this will allow you to visit the different locations. At the end of the book, I have included a table with recommendations that include, in my opinion, the best time of the year and time of the day to visit them.

Location Information

Location	What to See!	Time of Year	Time of Day
Mono Lake	Tufa, Osprey, Eastern Sierras	Early May	Golden Hours
Lundy Canyon	Stream, Beaver, Beaver, Dam, Waterfall, Wildflowers	April/May	Late Afternoon
Chemung Gold Mine	Gold Mine Ruins	May to October	Golden Hour
Bodie State Park	Historical Town and Gold Mine	May/August	Golden Hour
Death Valley National Monument	Canyons, Sand Dunes, Darwin Falls, Scottie's Castle	April to October	Golden Hour
Alabama Hills	Rock Canyons, Arches, Mount Whitney	May to October	Golden Hour
Yosemite National Park	Waterfalls, Wildlife, Wildflowers, Forest	April to November	Golden Hour
Sacramento National Wildlife Refuge	Bald Eagles, Snow Geese, Hawks, Wildlife	Mid-January	Morning
Colusa Wildlife Refuge	Snow Geese, Ghost Herons, Owls, Deer, Hawks	Mid-January	Morning

Location	Features	When	Time
Lassen Volcanic National Park	Waterfalls, Lakes, Streams, Meadows, Hot Springs	July to September	Golden Hour
Hat Creek-Burney Falls Area-Pit River	Streams, Waterfalls, Lakes, Wildlife	June to October	Golden Hour
McCloud River Recreational Area	3 Waterfalls, Landscape, Butterflies	June to September	Golden Hour
Dunsmuir Area	Hedge Creek Falls, Butterflies, Wildflowers, Mossbrae Falls	April to August	Early Morning
Point Reyes National Seashore	Elk--Pierce Ranch	October/November	Early Morning
Point Reyes National Seashore	Elephant Seals--Boat House	March/April	Early Morning
Point Reyes National Seashore	Wildflowers---Abbotts Lagoon & Chimney Rock	March to June	Golden Hour
Point Reyes National Seashore	Landscape, Deer-Earthquake Walk and Chimney Rock	All Year Round	Golden Hour
Point Reyes National Seashore	Birds--Abbotts Lagoon & Limantour Beach	September to February	Golden Hour
Muir Woods	Lady Bugs, Mushrooms,	February	Golden Hour

National Monument	Redwoods, and Landscape		
Santa Cruz Area	Monarch Butterflies	October	11am
Santa Cruz Area	Hummingbirds - Flowers	March/April/May	9am
Elkhorn Slough	Sea Otters, Birds and Harbor Seals	June to September	Scheduled Tour
Hallberg Butterfly Garden	Pipevine Swallowtails, Birds, and Other Butterflies	April/May	Morning
Ironstone Winery	Flowers, Vineyards, Gold Mine Equipment	March	Morning
Uvas Canyon Regional Parks	Waterfalls, Ferns, Streams, Oaks, and Lady Bugs	March	Golden Hour
Carson Pass Area	Lakes, Waterfalls, Wildflowers, Cabins and Gold Mine	June to October	Golden Hour

www.ingramcontent.com/pod-product-compliance
Lightning Source LLC
Chambersburg PA
CBHW050254220526
45465CB00002B/679